Spectrum Test Prep

Grade 1

Test Preparation for:

Reading
Language
Math

Program Authors:
Dale I. Foreman
S. Alan Cohen
Jerome D. Kaplan
Ruth Mitchell

Table of Contents

1-57768-101-0

Spectrum Test Prep
The Program That Teaches Test-Taking Achievement

For over two decades, McGraw-Hill has helped students perform their best when taking standardized achievement tests. Over the years, we have identified the skills and strategies that students need to master the challenges of taking a standardized test. Becoming familiar with the test-taking experience can help ensure your child's success.

Spectrum Test Prep covers all test skill areas

Spectrum Test Prep contains the subject areas that are represented in the five major standardized tests. *Spectrum Test Prep* will help your child prepare for the following tests:

- California Achievement Tests® (CAT/5)
- Comprehensive Tests of Basic Skills (CTBS/4)
- Iowa Tests of Basic Skills® (ITBS, Form K)
- Metropolitan Achievement Test (MAT/7)
- Stanford Achievement Test (SAT/9)

Spectrum Test Prep provides strategies for success

Many students need special support when preparing to take a standardized test. *Spectrum Test Prep* gives your child the opportunity to practice and become familiar with:

- General test content
- The test format
- Listening and following standard directions
- Working in structured settings
- Maintaining a silent, sustained effort
- Using test-taking strategies

Spectrum Test Prep is comprehensive

Spectrum Test Prep provides a complete presentation of the types of skills covered in standardized tests in a variety of formats. These formats are similar to those your child will encounter when testing. The subject areas covered in this book include:

- Reading
- Language
- Math

Spectrum Test Prep gives students the practice they need

Each student lesson provides several components that help develop test-taking skills:

- An **Example,** with directions and sample test items
- A **Tips** feature, that gives test-taking strategies
- A **Practice** section, to help students practice answering questions in each test format

Each book gives focused test practice that builds confidence:

- A **Test Yourself** lesson for each unit gives students the opportunity to apply what they have learned in the unit.
- A **Test Practice** section gives students the experience of a longer test-like situation.
- A **Progress Chart** allows students to note and record their own progress.

Spectrum Test Prep is the first and most successful program ever developed to help students become familiar with the test-taking experience. *Spectrum Test Prep* can help to build self-confidence, reduce test anxiety, and provide the opportunity for students to successfully show what they have learned.

A Message to Parents and Teachers:

- **Standardized tests: the yardstick for your child's future**

    Standardized testing is one of the cornerstones of American education. From its beginning in the early part of this century, standardized testing has gradually become the yardstick by which student performance is judged. For better or worse, your child's future will be determined in great part by how well she or he performs on the standardized test used by your school district.

- **Even good students can have trouble with testing**

    In general, standardized tests are well designed and carefully developed to assess students' abilities in a consistent and balanced manner. However, there are many factors that can hinder the performance of an individual student when testing. These might include test anxiety, unfamiliarity with the test's format, or failing to understand the directions.

    In addition, it is rare that students are taught all of the material that appears on a standardized test. This is because the curriculum of most schools does not directly match the content of the standardized test. There will certainly be overlap between what your child learns in school and how he or she is tested, but some materials will probably be unfamiliar.

- **Ready to Test will lend a helping hand**

    It is because of the shortcomings of the standardized testing process that *Spectrum Test Prep* was developed. The lessons in the book were created after a careful analysis of the most popular achievement tests. The items, while different from those on the tests, reflect the types of material that your child will encounter when testing. Students who use *Spectrum Test Prep* will also become familiar with the format of the most popular achievement tests. This learning experience will reduce anxiety and give your child the opportunity to do his or her best on the next standardized test.

We urge you to review with your child the Message to Students and the feature "How to Use This Book" on pages 6-8. The information on these pages will help your child to use this book and develop important test-taking skills. We are confident that following the recommendations in this book will help your child to earn a test score that accurately reflects his or her true ability.

A Message to Students:

Frequently in school you will be asked to take a standardized achievement test. This test will show how much you know compared to other students in your grade. Your score on a standardized achievement test will help your teachers plan your education. It will also give you and your parents an idea of what your learning strengths and weaknesses are.

This book will help you do your best on a standardized achievement test. It will show you what to expect on the test and will give you a chance to practice important reading and test-taking skills. Here are some suggestions you can follow to make the best use of *Spectrum Test Prep*.

Plan for success
- You'll do your best if you begin studying and do one or two lessons in this book each week. If you only have a little bit of time before a test is given, you can do one or two lessons each day.
- Study a little bit at a time, no more than 30 minutes a day. If you can, choose the same time each day to study in a quiet place.
- Keep a record of your score on each lesson. The charts on pp. 160–162 of this book will help you do this.

On the day of the test . . .
- Get a good night's sleep the night before the test. Have a light breakfast and lunch to keep from feeling drowsy during the test.
- Use the tips you learned in *Spectrum Test Prep*. The most important tips are to skip difficult items, take the best guess when you're unsure of the answer, and try all the items.
- Don't worry if you are a little nervous when you take an achievement test. This is a natural feeling and may even help you stay alert.

How to Use This Book

1 Getting Started

Read the directions carefully.

Do the Sample item(s).

Read the Tips(s).

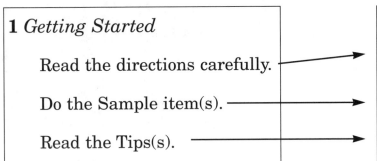

2 Practice

Complete the Practice items.

Continue working until you reach a Stop sign.

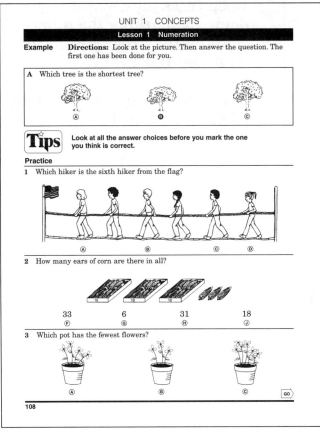

UNIT 1   CONCEPTS

Lesson 1   Numeration

Example   **Directions:** Look at the picture. Then answer the question. The first one has been done for you.

A   Which tree is the shortest tree?

Ⓐ   Ⓑ   Ⓒ

Tips   Look at all the answer choices before you mark the one you think is correct.

Practice

1   Which hiker is the sixth hiker from the flag?

Ⓐ   Ⓑ   Ⓒ   Ⓓ

2   How many ears of corn are there in all?

33   6   31   18
Ⓕ   Ⓖ   Ⓗ   Ⓙ

3   Which pot has the fewest flowers?

Ⓐ   Ⓑ   Ⓒ   GO

108

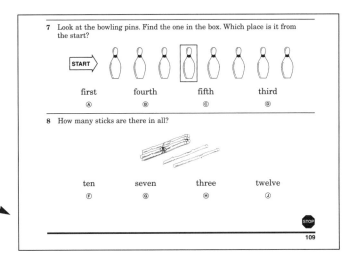

7   Look at the bowling pins. Find the one in the box. Which place is it from the start?

START

first   fourth   fifth   third
Ⓐ   Ⓑ   Ⓒ   Ⓓ

8   How many sticks are there in all?

ten   seven   three   twelve
Ⓕ   Ⓖ   Ⓗ   Ⓙ

STOP

109

3 Check It Out

Check your answers by turning to the Answer Key at the back of the book.

Keep track of how you're doing by marking the number right on the Progress Charts on pages 160-162.

Mark the lesson you completed on the table of contents for each section.

Answer Key

Reading	C A		6 F		6 H		
Unit 1,	D G		7 C		7 C		
Word Analysis	1 B		8 G		8 G		
Lesson 1–pg. 12	2 F		9 C		9 A		
A A	3 C		10 G		10 H		
1 D	4 G		11 C		11 C		
2 H	5 C		12 F		12 G		
3 D	6 G				13 A		
4 F	7 C		Lesson 11–pg. 24		14 G		
5 B	8 G		A A		15 C		
6 F	9 C		B H		16 F		
	10 J		1 D		17 B		
Lesson 2–pg. 13	11 C		2 G		18 F		
A B	12 F		3 A		19 D		
1 C			4 J		20 H		
2 F	Lesson 8–pgs. 19–21		5 C		21 C		
3 D	A B		6 G		22 G		
4 H	B J		7 D		23 A		
	C C				24 F		
Lesson 3–pg. 14	D F		Lesson 12–pg. 25		25 D		
A A	1 C		A A		26 H		
B J	2 G		B F		27 A		
C C	3 A		1 B		28 G		
1 B	4 H		2 H		29 B		
2 F	5 B		3 D		30 J		
3 D	6 D		4 G		31 A		
4 G	7 D		5 C		32 F		
5 C	8 C		6 F				
	9 C				Unit 3,		
Lesson 4–pg. 15	10 J		Lesson 13–pg. 26		Reading Comprehension		
A B	11 C		A A		Lesson 16–pg. 32		
1 C	12 B		B F		A C		
2 F	13 B		1 D		1 A		
3 B	14 F		2 H		2 H		
	15 B		3 A		3 B		
Lesson 5–pg. 16	16 F		4 G				
A A	17 C		5 A		Lesson 17–pg. 33		
B H	18 G		6 J		A B		
1 C					2 H		
2 G	Unit 2,		Lesson 14–pg. 27		3 B		
3 D	Vocabulary		A A		4 H		
4 F	Lesson 9–pg. 22		B J				
5 D	A C		1 C		Lesson 18–pg. 34		
6 G	1 B		2 G		A B		
	2 G		4 H		B H		
Lesson 6–pg. 17	3 C				1 A		
A C	4 F		Lesson 15–pgs. 28–31		2 G		
B F			A C		3 A		
1 B	Lesson 10–pg. 23		B G		4 H		
2 F	A C		C A				
3 D	B F		1 B		Lesson 19–pgs. 35–38		
4 G	1 B		2 H		A B		
5 C	2 F		3 A		1 A		
	3 C		4 F		2 H		
Lesson 7–pg. 18	4 F		5 A		3 A		
A B	5 B						
B H							

155

Reading Progress Chart

Circle your score for each lesson. Connect your scores to see how well you are doing.

Unit 1								Unit 2							Unit 3				
Lesson 1	Lesson 2	Lesson 3	Lesson 4	Lesson 5	Lesson 6	Lesson 7	Lesson 8	Lesson 9	Lesson 10	Lesson 11	Lesson 12	Lesson 13	Lesson 14	Lesson 15	Lesson 16	Lesson 17	Lesson 18	Lesson 19	Lesson 20
6	4	5	3	6	5	12	18	4	12	7	6	6	4	32	3	4	4	13	10

160

Table of Contents
Reading

11

Skills

Reading

WORD ANALYSIS

Matching a letter to its spoken name
Identifying the initial letter of a word
Identifying words with matching beginning sounds
Identifying final consonant sounds
Identifying rhyming words
Identifying words with matching vowel sounds
Identifying medial vowel sounds

Identifying sight words
Identifying compound words
Recognizing suffixes
Recognizing contractions
Matching phonemes
Identifying initial consonant sounds
Forming words from structural clues

VOCABULARY

Matching pictures and oral/written statements
Identifying words associated with a picture
Identifying synonyms

Identifying antonyms
Identifying words in context

READING COMPREHENSION

Understanding oral stories
Identifying the sentence to go with a picture
Understanding sentence meaning
Sequencing ideas
Understanding characters
Recognizing details
Understanding the author's purpose

Drawing conclusions
Making inferences
Understanding the main idea
Understanding feelings
Predicting outcomes
Identifying story genre
Deriving word or phrase meaning

Language

LISTENING

Matching a picture to an orally presented or
    written scenario
Choosing a printed answer to an orally presented
    or written scenario

Classifying a picture in response to an orally
    presented or written scenario

LANGUAGE MECHANICS

Identifying the need for capital letters (proper
    nouns, beginning words, pronoun I) in
    sentences
Identifying the need for punctuation marks
    (period, question mark, exclamation
    point, apostrophe) in sentences

Identifying the need for capital letters and
    punctuation marks in printed text

LANGUAGE EXPRESSION

Identifying the correct forms of nouns, verbs,
    and adjectives
Identifying the correct forms of pronouns
Forming a question from a declarative sentence

Identifying correctly formed sentences
Identifying the correct sentence to complete
    a paragraph

SPELLING

Identifying correctly spelled words
Identifying incorrectly spelled words

STUDY SKILLS

Alphabetizing words
Using a table of contents
Prewriting

Math

COMPUTATION

Adding whole numbers

Subtracting whole numbers

CONCEPTS

Associating number words with objects
Associating numerals with number words
Associating numerals with objects
Comparing and ordering whole numbers
Counting
Determining ordinal position
Identifying fractional parts
Matching groups of objects

Recognizing numerals
Recognizing visual and numeric patterns
Sequencing
Skip counting
Understanding place value
Understanding terminology
Using expanded notation

APPLICATIONS

Differentiating among measuring instruments
Matching shapes
Reading a calendar
Recognizing plane and solid figures and their
    characteristics
Recognizing value of coins
Solving oral and written word problems

Telling time
Understanding bar graphs and pictographs
Understanding congruence and symmetry
Understanding elapsed time
Understanding spatial relations
Using non-standard units of measurement
Using standard and metric units of measurement

—————— Strategies ——————

Following group directions
Adjusting to a structured setting
Listening carefully
Utilizing test formats
Maintaining a silent, sustained effort
Locating questions and answer choices
Following oral and/or written directions
Taking the best guess when unsure of the answer
Comparing answer choices
Considering every answer choice
Subvocalizing answer choices
Working methodically
Following complex directions
Marking the right answer as soon as it is found
Focusing on the defined task
Skipping difficult items and returning to
    them later
Referring to a picture to find the answer
Understanding unusual item formats
Recalling oral and/or written information
Staying with the first answer
Using context to find the answer
Substituting answer choices
Inferring word meaning from context

Using key words to find the answer
Using logic
Eliminating answer choices
Skimming a passage
Referring to a passage to answer questions
Managing time effectively
Locating the correct answer
Indicating that an item has no mistakes
Trying out answer choices
Recalling the elements of a correctly
    formed sentence
Recalling the elements of a correctly
    formed paragraph
Recalling the spelling of familiar words
Referring to a reference source
Computing carefully
Converting problems to a workable format
Finding the answer without computing
Identifying and using key words, figures,
    and numbers
Identifying the best test-taking strategy
Listening to information presented orally
Saying answer choices to yourself

Table of Contents
Reading

Example Choose the best answers to the questions. The first one has been done for you. Do numbers 1-6 the same way.

Which letter does the word "ring" begin with?

A   r   c   m   s
     Ⓐ   Ⓑ   Ⓒ   Ⓓ

Tips If you are not sure which answer is correct, take your best guess.

Practice

Which letter does the word "hand" begin with?

    l   t   n   h
1   Ⓐ   Ⓑ   Ⓒ   Ⓓ

Which letter does the word "fun" begin with?

    u   i   f   b
2   Ⓕ   Ⓖ   Ⓗ   Ⓙ

Which letter does the word "van" begin with?

    s   o   w   v
3   Ⓐ   Ⓑ   Ⓒ   Ⓓ

Which letter does the word "day" begin with?

    d   p   q   b
4   Ⓕ   Ⓖ   Ⓗ   Ⓙ

Which letter does the word "nose" begin with?

    a   n   e   u
5   Ⓐ   Ⓑ   Ⓒ   Ⓓ

Which letter does the word "kite" begin with?

    k   b   y   p
6   Ⓕ   Ⓖ   Ⓗ   Ⓙ

STOP

Example   **Directions:** Look at the picture on the side of the page. Now look at the words next to the picture. Find the word that begins with the same beginning sound as the one in the picture.

A   The first one has been done for you.

present

tent	price	frost	seven
Ⓐ	⬤Ⓑ	Ⓒ	Ⓓ

Tips   Say the name of the picture to yourself. Then say each of the answer choices.

Do numbers 1-4 the same way.
Practice

1

pair	reach	cheek	sled
Ⓐ	Ⓑ	Ⓒ	Ⓓ

2

star	pool	hill	glad
Ⓕ	Ⓖ	Ⓗ	Ⓙ

3

get	land	tag	bell
Ⓐ	Ⓑ	Ⓒ	Ⓓ

4

shove	blue	glass	vase
Ⓕ	Ⓖ	Ⓗ	Ⓙ

Examples **Directions:** Look at the word on the side of the page. For A, look at the pictures next to the word. Find the word in the row beside the picture that has the same ending sound as the word on the side of the page. The first one has been done for you. For Band C, look at the word on the side of the page, then find the word in the row that has the same ending sound. Do numbers 1-5 the same way.

A

hop   Ⓐ   Ⓑ   Ⓒ

B   Practice on these.

	back	sad	not	cab
rib	Ⓕ	Ⓖ	Ⓗ	Ⓙ

C	han<u>d</u>	gif<u>t</u>	rin<u>g</u>
hang	Ⓐ	Ⓑ	Ⓒ

Tips   **Listen carefully and think about the ending sounds of the words.**

Practice
1

poor Ⓐ   Ⓑ    Ⓒ

2	spin	rake	nest	snow
rain	Ⓕ	Ⓖ	Ⓗ	Ⓙ

3	light	spin	tall	have
love	Ⓐ	Ⓑ	Ⓒ	Ⓓ

4	han<u>g</u>	ten<u>t</u>	rus<u>t</u>
hunt	Ⓕ	Ⓖ	Ⓗ

5	thic<u>k</u>	an<u>t</u>	ar<u>m</u>
form	Ⓐ	Ⓑ	Ⓒ

STOP

Example   **Directions:** Look at the word on the side of the page. Which picture rhymes with that word? This one has been done for you. Do numbers 1-3 the same way.

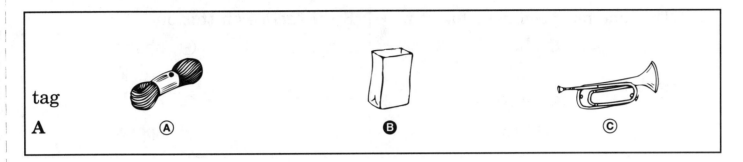

tag
A   Ⓐ   Ⓑ   Ⓒ

 Look at the pictures while you say the word to yourself.
Listen for the ending sound.

Practice

smart
1   Ⓐ   Ⓑ   Ⓒ

moon
2   Ⓕ   Ⓖ   Ⓗ

flip
3   Ⓐ   Ⓑ   Ⓒ

Examples   **Directions:** Say the word on the left side of the box. Look at the underlined part of the word. Now find the word in the column that has the same sound as the underlined part.

A This one has been done for you.	B Practice on this one.
tr<u>u</u>ck Ⓐ but Ⓑ oil Ⓒ stiff Ⓓ mile	**f<u>ou</u>nd** Ⓕ show Ⓖ stuck Ⓗ cow Ⓙ spend

Do numbers 1-6 the same way.

 If an item is too hard, skip it and come back to it later.

Practice

1

l<u>i</u>ne
- Ⓐ juice
- Ⓑ pound
- Ⓒ kind
- Ⓓ ruin

4

r<u>ea</u>ch
- Ⓕ here
- Ⓖ chair
- Ⓗ best
- Ⓙ branch

2

ch<u>oi</u>ce
- Ⓕ close
- Ⓖ spoil
- Ⓗ flood
- Ⓙ cloth

5

h<u>o</u>pe
- Ⓐ chop
- Ⓑ spoon
- Ⓒ hair
- Ⓓ float

3

p<u>e</u>t
- Ⓐ bring
- Ⓑ hair
- Ⓒ chip
- Ⓓ send

6

b<u>oo</u>t
- Ⓕ bone
- Ⓖ smooth
- Ⓗ trap
- Ⓙ tub

STOP

Examples   **Directions:** Choose the best answer to the question. The first one has been done for you. Practice on the second one.

A What word has the same vowel sound as the picture?

bad
(A)

get
(B)

may
●C

leg
(D)

B What word has the same vowel as "code"?

rode
(F)

ride
(G)

rose
(H)

hope
(J)

Do numbers 1-5 the same way.

Tips   **Look at each choice before you mark your answer.**

Practice

1   What word has the same vowel sound as the picture?

long
(A)

food
(B)

spot
(C)

house
(D)

2   What word has the same vowel sound as the picture?

miss
(F)

mind
(G)

boil
(H)

rain
(J)

3   What word means the opposite of "over"?

until
(A)

send
(B)

after
(C)

under
(D)

4   What word rhymes with "bell?"

seal
(F)

sell
(G)

seem
(H)

field
(J)

5   What word rhymes with "smart"?

make
(A)

post
(B)

part
(C)

trap
(D)

STOP

Directions: Look at each of the three words in the line. Which one has a word that is really two words? The first one has been done for you.

Example

A	window	sidewalk	cleaning
	Ⓐ	●	Ⓒ

Do numbers 1-3 the same way.

Tips Read or listen carefully to the directions. Be sure your answer matches the directions.

Practice

1 feather notebook purple
   Ⓐ   Ⓑ   Ⓒ

2 horseshoe ringing kitchen
   Ⓕ   Ⓖ   Ⓗ

3 letter warning armchair
   Ⓐ   Ⓑ   Ⓒ

Directions: What word completes the sentence? The first one has been done for you. Do numbers 4-9 the same way.

Example The store is not open. It is _____.

B	closest	closed	closer
	Ⓕ	Ⓖ	Ⓗ

4 lands landing landed
   Ⓕ   Ⓖ   Ⓗ

5 nicely nicest nicer
   Ⓐ   Ⓑ   Ⓒ

6 even ever evening
   Ⓕ   Ⓖ   Ⓗ

Directions: Read the sentence and look at the underlined words. Find the shortened form of the words and mark the correct choice. Practice on this one. Then do numbers 7-9 the same way.

Example <u>She will</u> be here soon.

C	she'll	she's	she'd
	Ⓐ	Ⓑ	Ⓒ

They <u>do not</u> live here.

7 doesn't didn't don't
   Ⓐ   Ⓑ   Ⓒ

I <u>was not</u> happy.

8 weren't wasn't won't
   Ⓕ   Ⓖ   Ⓗ

I'm sorry <u>we are</u> late.

9 we'll we've we're
   Ⓐ   Ⓑ   Ⓒ

Directions: Say the word above each line. Look at the underlined part. Which word has the same sound as the underlined part? The first one has been done for you. Do numbers 10-12 the same way.

Example

D b<u>o</u>th	hop	rope	for
	Ⓕ	Ⓖ	Ⓗ

10 **tr<u>i</u>p** thick train smart
   Ⓕ   Ⓖ   Ⓗ

11 **fl<u>ew</u>** were weed shoe
   Ⓐ   Ⓑ   Ⓒ

12 **b<u>ir</u>d** order drink dark
   Ⓕ   Ⓖ   Ⓗ

STOP

Directions: Choose the best answers for each question. The first one has been done for you.

Example A What picture starts with the same sound as "meet"?

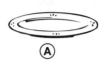
Ⓐ

Ⓑ

Ⓒ

Example B Practice on this one. What word starts with the same sound as "hill"?

boat	meat	side	hope
Ⓕ	Ⓖ	Ⓗ	Ⓙ

Do numbers 1-5 the same way.

1 What picture begins with the same sound as "heat"?

Ⓐ

Ⓑ

Ⓒ

---

2 What word begins with the same sound as the one in the picture?

big	wet	saw	yes
Ⓕ	Ⓖ	Ⓗ	Ⓙ

---

3 What letters represent the same beginning sound as the one in the picture?

tr	nt	dr
Ⓐ	Ⓑ	Ⓒ

---

4 What word begins with the same sound as "goat"?

tape	leg	girl	moon
Ⓕ	Ⓖ	Ⓗ	Ⓙ

---

5 What word begins with the same sound as "clock"?

crab	clap	slip
Ⓐ	Ⓑ	Ⓒ

19

Directions: Look at the word on the side of the page. Look at the underlined part. Which word has the same sound as the underlined part?

Example C This one has been done for you.	**Example D** Practice on this one.
chase (A) chin (B) dark (C) rain (D) sand	fl<u>y</u> (F) high (G) yes (H) study (J) bait

Do numbers 1-13 the same way.

6

tr<u>a</u>p
- (F) had
- (G) trial
- (H) chain
- (J) park

7

st<u>ea</u>m
- (A) base
- (B) met
- (C) last
- (D) cheese

8

l<u>e</u>t
- (F) deep
- (G) rest
- (H) tail
- (J) leak

9

<u>ch</u>eer
- (A) check
- (B) bench
- (C) piece
- (D) head

10

t<u>ou</u>ch
- (F) reach
- (G) toast
- (H) pound
- (J) lunch

11

n<u>oo</u>n
- (A) note
- (B) open
- (C) blue
- (D) loud

12

sm<u>i</u>le
- (F) dial
- (G) small
- (H) miss
- (J) sail

13

dr<u>i</u>nk
- (A) dark
- (B) hidden
- (C) bank
- (D) roast

STOP

Directions: Look at the picture. It is a picture of a pear. If we took the first letter away and replaced it with a "b," what would the word say? Choose the picture that shows that word.

14   b   Ⓕ   Ⓖ   Ⓗ

Do this one the same way.

15   v   Ⓐ   Ⓑ   Ⓒ

Directions: Choose the beginning sound that will form the word shown in the picture. Do numbers 16–18 the same way.

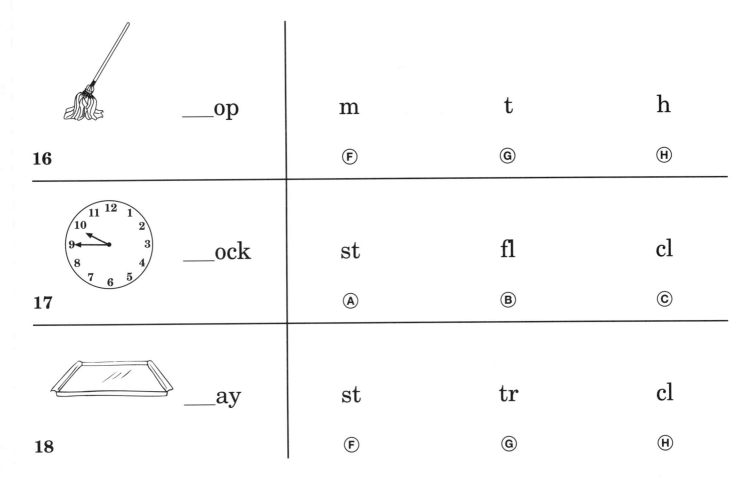

16   ___op

m   Ⓕ   t   Ⓖ   h   Ⓗ

17   ___ock

st   Ⓐ   fl   Ⓑ   cl   Ⓒ

18   ___ay

st   Ⓕ   tr   Ⓖ   cl   Ⓗ

STOP

Lesson 9 Picture Vocabulary

Example   **Directions:** Find the picture that completes each sentence. This one has been done for you. Do numbers 1-4 the same way.

A   Put the books on the _____.

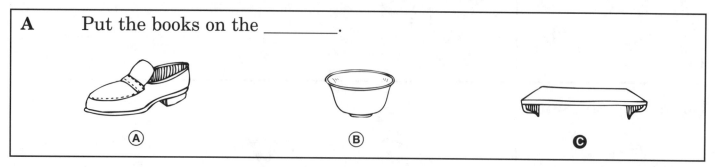

Ⓐ   Ⓑ   Ⓒ

 Read or listen carefully. Think about what you hear while you look at the pictures.

Practice

1   I sleep on a _____.

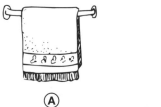   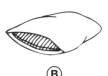

Ⓐ   Ⓑ   Ⓒ

2   The _____ comes from a bird.

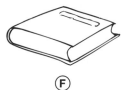      

Ⓕ   Ⓖ   Ⓗ

3   The girl wearing gym shoes is _____.

Ⓐ   Ⓑ   Ⓒ

4   The _____ is beside the fireplace.

Ⓕ   Ⓖ   Ⓗ

Examples   **Directions:** Look at the picture. What word in each group matches the picture? This one has been done for you.

A	dog	bird	cat
	Ⓐ	Ⓑ	**Ⓒ**

Practice on this one.

B	fur	fly	bark
	Ⓕ	Ⓖ	Ⓗ

 **Tips**   **Look at the answer choices then look back at the picture.**

Do numbers 1-12 the same way.

Practice

1	game	secret	away		7	belt	under	drive
	Ⓐ	Ⓑ	Ⓒ			Ⓐ	Ⓑ	Ⓒ

2	tell	find	chase		8	shoes	tires	drops
	Ⓕ	Ⓖ	Ⓗ			Ⓕ	Ⓖ	Ⓗ

3	reads	marks	friends		9	wagon	plane	camper
	Ⓐ	Ⓑ	Ⓒ			Ⓐ	Ⓑ	Ⓒ

4	candle	room	cold		10	night	family	main
	Ⓕ	Ⓖ	Ⓗ			Ⓕ	Ⓖ	Ⓗ

5	table	flame	dime		11	band	pen	meal
	Ⓐ	Ⓑ	Ⓒ			Ⓐ	Ⓑ	Ⓒ

6	light	sky	reach		12	eat	rush	horse
	Ⓕ	Ⓖ	Ⓗ			Ⓕ	Ⓖ	Ⓗ

STOP

Examples   **Directions:** Find the word that matches each phrase. This one has been done for you.

	to look for . . .			
A	search	help	build	cover
	Ⓐ	Ⓑ	Ⓒ	Ⓓ

	something hard . . .			
B	cloth	water	wood	hair
	Ⓕ	Ⓖ	Ⓗ	Ⓙ

 **Tips**   **Once you have marked your answer, don't change it.**

Do numbers 1-7 the same way.
Practice

	something you can cross . . .			
1	plane	cloud	wave	bridge
	Ⓐ	Ⓑ	Ⓒ	Ⓓ

	something you can listen to . . .			
2	plate	radio	window	chair
	Ⓕ	Ⓖ	Ⓗ	Ⓙ

	to eat a little . . .			
3	snack	nap	play	sting
	Ⓐ	Ⓑ	Ⓒ	Ⓓ

	to control a car . . .			
4	buy	repair	leave	steer
	Ⓕ	Ⓖ	Ⓗ	Ⓙ

	a place where people live . . .			
5	park	store	house	train
	Ⓐ	Ⓑ	Ⓒ	Ⓓ

	a noise a cat makes . . .			
6	chase	purr	warm	bark
	Ⓕ	Ⓖ	Ⓗ	Ⓙ

	a vegetable . . .			
7	bake	shop	dinner	potato
	Ⓐ	Ⓑ	Ⓒ	Ⓓ

STOP

Examples   **Directions:** Find the word that means the same thing as the underlined word.

The first one has been done for you.	Practice on this one.
A We saw a large <u>boat</u>.	**B The <u>stack</u> of papers is heavy.**
Ⓐ truck	Ⓕ pile
Ⓑ fish	Ⓖ box
Ⓒ car	Ⓗ bag
Ⓓ ship	Ⓙ pair

 **The meaning of the sentence will help you find the right answer.**

Do numbers 1-6 the same way.
Practice

1   This <u>street</u> is busy.

Ⓐ store

Ⓑ road

Ⓒ house

Ⓓ bank

2   Cindy found a pretty <u>rock</u>.

Ⓕ flower

Ⓖ tree

Ⓗ stone

Ⓙ lake

3   They had to <u>hurry</u> home.

Ⓐ fly

Ⓑ drive

Ⓒ leave

Ⓓ rush

4   The movie was <u>great</u>.

Ⓕ bad

Ⓖ wonderful

Ⓗ long

Ⓙ dull

5   Can you <u>fix</u> the bike?

Ⓐ break

Ⓑ buy

Ⓒ repair

Ⓓ find

6   The eagle was near the <u>middle</u> of the lake.

Ⓕ center

Ⓖ edge

Ⓗ side

Ⓙ surface

Examples **Directions:** Find the word that means the opposite of the underlined word.

The first one has been done for you.	Practice on this one.
A Randy was on the <u>lowest</u> step.	**B The book was too <u>short</u>.**
Ⓐ highest	Ⓕ long
Ⓑ widest	Ⓖ sad
Ⓒ middle	Ⓗ heavy
Ⓓ broken	Ⓙ boring

 **Remember, the right answer will mean the <u>opposite</u> of the underlined word.**

Do numbers 1-6 the same way.
Practice

1 We can <u>return</u> later.

Ⓐ play

Ⓑ study

Ⓒ travel

Ⓓ leave

2 Lynn <u>threw</u> the ball.

Ⓕ dropped

Ⓖ found

Ⓗ caught

Ⓙ bought

3 Yesterday was very <u>rainy</u>.

Ⓐ sunny

Ⓑ cold

Ⓒ windy

Ⓓ cloudy

4 D'wayne <u>bought</u> a can of juice.

Ⓕ dropped

Ⓖ sold

Ⓗ found

Ⓙ drank

5 <u>Many</u> animals live in our park.

Ⓐ few

Ⓑ wild

Ⓒ funny

Ⓓ small

6 Is that coat <u>new</u>?

Ⓕ yours

Ⓖ hers

Ⓗ warm

Ⓙ old

Examples   **Directions:** Find the word that means the same thing as the underlined word. This one has been done for you. Do numbers 1 and 2 the same way.

A <u>rich</u> family

- Ⓐ **wealthy**
- Ⓑ friendly
- Ⓒ kind
- Ⓓ nearby

B We went on a _____ to the beach. It took us two hours to get there.

- Ⓕ swim
- Ⓖ sand
- Ⓗ park
- Ⓙ trip

Directions: Find the word that completes each sentence. The first one has been done for you. Do numbers 3 and 4 the same way.

 **As soon as you know which answer is correct, mark it and get ready for the next item.**

Practice

1   <u>noisy</u> party

- Ⓐ large
- Ⓑ surprise
- Ⓒ loud
- Ⓓ crowded

2   <u>enjoy</u> fishing

- Ⓕ go
- Ⓖ like
- Ⓗ remember
- Ⓙ lend

3   It was a great play. We began to _____ our hands as soon as it was over.

- Ⓐ leave
- Ⓑ clap
- Ⓒ wash
- Ⓓ hold

4   Put the food on the _____ and carry it to the table.

- Ⓕ floor
- Ⓖ store
- Ⓗ dish

STOP   **STOP**

Example A   **Directions:** Look at the word or phrase. Find the picture that shows what the word means. Practice on this one.

A warm jacket

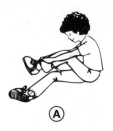
Ⓐ

Ⓑ

Ⓒ

Do numbers 1-4 the same way.

A fortress

1   Ⓐ   Ⓑ   Ⓒ

A bright light

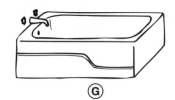

2   Ⓕ   Ⓖ   Ⓗ

A girl leaping

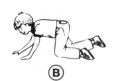

3   Ⓐ   Ⓑ   Ⓒ

A sorrowful girl

4   Ⓕ   Ⓖ   Ⓗ

STOP

Directions: Find the word in each line that goes with the picture. The first two have been done for you. Do numbers 5-16 the same way.

Example B

coat	scarf	hat
Ⓕ	**Ⓖ**	Ⓗ

Example C

neck	foot	arm
Ⓐ	Ⓑ	Ⓒ

5
tools	toys	books
Ⓐ	Ⓑ	Ⓒ

6
run	fly	dig
Ⓕ	Ⓖ	Ⓗ

7
floor	kitchen	yard
Ⓐ	Ⓑ	Ⓒ

11
drop	carry	write
Ⓐ	Ⓑ	Ⓒ

12
floor	letter	shoe
Ⓕ	Ⓖ	Ⓗ

13
pen	car	bus
Ⓐ	Ⓑ	Ⓒ

8
write	paint	read
Ⓕ	Ⓖ	Ⓗ

9
brush	spoon	comb
Ⓐ	Ⓑ	Ⓒ

10
sky	dirt	color
Ⓕ	Ⓖ	Ⓗ

14
team	boy	lake
Ⓕ	Ⓖ	Ⓗ

15
sit	jump	fly
Ⓐ	Ⓑ	Ⓒ

16
kite	ball	stick
Ⓕ	Ⓖ	Ⓗ

STOP

Directions: Find the word that means the same thing as the underlined word. Do numbers 17-20 the same way.

17 The bear was huge.

- Ⓐ small
- Ⓑ large
- Ⓒ furry
- Ⓓ hungry

18 I liked that part of the book.

- Ⓕ section
- Ⓖ cover
- Ⓗ page
- Ⓙ author

19 This is a hard game.

- Ⓐ easy
- Ⓑ fun
- Ⓒ long
- Ⓓ difficult

20 This coat is warm.

- Ⓕ hat
- Ⓖ shirt
- Ⓗ jacket
- Ⓙ cap

Directions: Find the word that means the opposite of the underlined word. Do numbers 21-24 the same way.

21 The room seems too dark.

- Ⓐ crowded
- Ⓑ small
- Ⓒ bright
- Ⓓ damp

22 Kim likes to save her money.

- Ⓕ count
- Ⓖ spend
- Ⓗ enjoy
- Ⓙ hide

23 We sold a tree.

- Ⓐ bought
- Ⓑ found
- Ⓒ want
- Ⓓ planted

24 The back of the room is cold.

- Ⓕ front
- Ⓖ side
- Ⓗ middle
- Ⓙ top

STOP

STOP

Read the phrase then find the word that means about the same as the underlined word. Do numbers 25 and 26 the same way.

25 notice a friend

Ⓐ forget

Ⓑ lose

Ⓒ race

Ⓓ see

26 become tired

Ⓕ awake

Ⓖ hungry

Ⓗ sleepy

Ⓙ lonely

Which word means the same as the underlined word? Do numbers 27 and 28 the same way.

27 slip on ice

Ⓐ slide

Ⓑ run

Ⓒ walk

Ⓓ turn

28 feel glad

Ⓕ music

Ⓖ happy

Ⓗ weak

Ⓙ silly

STOP

Find the word that will complete these sentences.

29 Both games are fun. I can't _____ which one to play with my friends.

Ⓐ agree

Ⓑ decide

Ⓒ find

Ⓓ begin

30 I dropped my watch. It fell to the _____ of the pond.

Ⓕ deep

Ⓖ beneath

Ⓗ top

Ⓙ bottom

31 The turtle walked _____ away from the children.

Ⓐ slowly

Ⓑ then

Ⓒ mildly

32 The weather is _____, so bring a sweater.

Ⓕ cool

Ⓖ outside

Ⓗ coming

STOP

Lesson 16   Listening Comprehension

Example   **Directions:** Read or listen to each story. Then choose the best answer to each question. The first one has been done for you. Do numbers 1-3 the same way.

A   Rita and her family were tired after the birthday party. They decided to order their dinner from the pizza shop rather than go to the grocery store. What did they order?

Ⓐ   Ⓑ   Ⓒ

   **Read or listen to the story. Think about the story when you try to answer the questions.**

Practice

1 Susan was going on vacation. Her family couldn't decide whether to go to the mountains, the desert, or the country. They decided to go to some place high. Where did they go?

   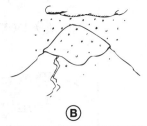   

Ⓐ   Ⓑ   Ⓒ

2 When they got to the mountains, it was cold. Susan put something on her head to keep her warm. Which one is Susan?

Ⓕ   Ⓖ   Ⓗ

3 Susan and her family saw a creature running through the snow. It was a creature that pulled a sled. You could also ride on its back. What was the creature?

Ⓐ   Ⓑ   Ⓒ

Example   **Directions:** Find the word that best describes the picture. The first one has been done for you.

A

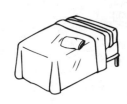

Ⓐ She slept too long.
🅑 The pillow is on the bed.
© The bed is messy.

Tips   **The right answer says the most about the picture.**

Do numbers 1-4 the same way.
Practice

1

Ⓐ Ryan likes his computer.
Ⓑ The boy likes to read.
© Nothing is on the desk.

2

Ⓕ It is too cold to swim.
Ⓖ The pool is crowded.
Ⓗ Louise dove into the pool.

3

Ⓐ The window is broken.
Ⓑ Mrs. Dean opened the window.
© The wind is blowing.

4

Ⓕ Laura and Tom are running.
Ⓖ The story is funny.
Ⓗ The children have a secret.

STOP

Examples   **Directions:** Read the word. Find the picture that matches the words or that completes the sentence.

The first one has been done for you.

A **This is made of metal.**
It is very light.

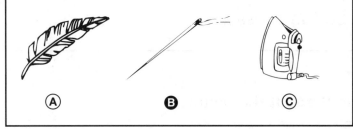

Ⓐ   Ⓑ   Ⓒ

Practice on this one.

B **This is a**

clock   time   watch
Ⓕ   Ⓖ   Ⓗ

   **Read the sentence. Think about what it means before you pick your answer.**

Do numbers 1-4 the same way.

Practice

1 **You can blow it.**
It makes noise.

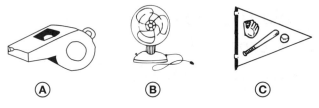

Ⓐ   Ⓑ   Ⓒ

2 **It is part of your arm.**
You can bend it.

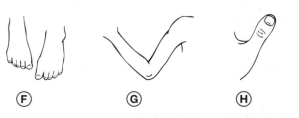

Ⓕ   Ⓖ   Ⓗ

3 **She is opening the**

window   door   box
Ⓐ   Ⓑ   Ⓒ

4 **Behind her is a**

bird   dog   cat
Ⓕ   Ⓖ   Ⓗ

STOP

Example

Directions: Read or listen to the story. Choose the best answers to the questions about the story. This one has been done for you. Do numbers 1-13 the same way.

The cat jumped up on the chair. She walked in a circle. Then she sat down. After a minute, she jumped down on the floor.

A **What did the cat do first?**

ⓐ Walked in a circle

🅑 Jumped up on the chair

ⓒ Sat down

 **Look back at the story to find the answer.**

Practice

The phone rang. Stan got up from the floor and answered it.

Stan talked to his mother for a minute. Then he ran into the garage and got his father. Mr. Miller put his tools down and came into the house.

1 **Who answered the phone?**

ⓐ Stan

ⓑ Stan's mother

ⓒ Stan's father

2 **Where was Mr. Miller?**

ⓕ At the office

ⓖ On the floor

ⓗ In the garage

GO

Directions: Read or listen to the story. Choose the best answers to the questions about the story.

Tugboats

A tugboat is small, but it does an important job. It helps big ships unload. Big ships carry things across the oceans. They have to go into harbors on the shore to unload. The big ships must sail into small places that they do not know well. They could run into something. The tugboat can push or pull the big ship safely into harbor. Tugs are strong and work very hard. A small tugboat can be sure a large ship gets into the harbor safely.

3 A tugboat is like a

Ⓐ helper.

Ⓑ harbor.

Ⓒ truck.

4 Tugboats make sure that ships are

Ⓕ fast.

Ⓖ big.

Ⓗ safe.

5 A tugboat's job is

Ⓐ silly.

Ⓑ important.

Ⓒ easy.

GO

Directions: Read or listen to the story. Choose the best answers to the questions about the story.

Do you eat well?

"It's time for lunch, boys." Mr. Little had made chicken sandwiches for Steve and Conroy. He had also put out a glass of milk and a piece of fruit for each boy. Mr. and Mrs. Little had eaten earlier.

"I wish we could have hamburgers and ice cream every day," said Steve. "I really don't like anything else."

"Wouldn't you get bored?" asked Conroy. "I sure would. Besides, all this different food is good for you. If you eat different things, you'll get bigger and stronger."

Steve looked at his older brother. Conroy was bigger and stronger, and Steve wanted to be just like his brother. He really liked Steve.

"Maybe you're right," answered Steve. "Does that mean I can't ever have hamburgers and ice cream and the other things I like?"

"Of course not." Conroy smiled at his little brother. "It's okay to have those things once in a while. But the better you eat, the faster you will grow. Maybe you'll be bigger than me pretty soon."

6 Who made lunch?

Ⓕ Mrs. Little

Ⓖ Mr. Little

Ⓗ Steve

7 Why was this story written?

Ⓐ To tell about eating right

Ⓑ To make you sad

Ⓒ To teach you how to cook

8 Why didn't Mr. and Mrs. Little eat with the boys?

Ⓕ They wanted hamburgers.

Ⓖ They weren't hungry.

Ⓗ They ate earlier.

9 Steve learned that

Ⓐ good food will help him grow bigger and stronger.

Ⓑ he can't ever eat ice cream again.

Ⓒ his big brother doesn't like hamburgers.

GO

Directions: Read or listen to the story. Choose the best answers to the questions about the story.

Have you ever seen a stethoscope?

When you go to the doctor, she will probably put something called a stethoscope on your chest. This instrument has a round piece of metal connected to rubber or plastic tubes. The doctor puts the tubes in her ears. This lets her hear your heart and lungs.

The stethoscope was invented by a French doctor named Rene Theophile around 1819. It was very different from the one that is used today. The modern stethoscope was invented by an American doctor named George Cammann.

Even though it is a simple tool, the stethoscope is very useful. It works so well that doctors can hear all kinds of different sounds inside your body. The stethoscope is used most often to listen to your heart. Sometimes a doctor will put a stethoscope on your chest or back. Then she will ask you to breathe deeply. Through the stethoscope, the doctor can hear the air going in and out of your lungs.

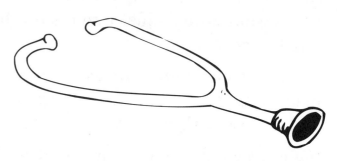

10 **Who invented the first stethoscope?**

Ⓕ George Cammann

Ⓖ Your doctor

Ⓗ A musician

Ⓙ Rene Theophile

11 **A doctor would probably put a stethoscope on your**

Ⓐ chest.

Ⓑ head.

Ⓒ arm.

Ⓓ leg.

12 **A stethoscope will work best in**

Ⓕ a noisy room.

Ⓖ a car.

Ⓗ a quiet room.

Ⓙ a loud office.

13 **Why was this story written?**

Ⓐ To answer a question

Ⓑ To tell about a medical tool

Ⓒ To tell about a famous person

Ⓓ To make you laugh

STOP

Directions: Find the picture that best matches the sentence. This one has been done for you. Do numbers 1-3 the same way.

Example A   Andrea found some money. She bent down to pick it up.

Ⓐ   Ⓑ   Ⓒ

Do this one the same way.

1   Peter's grandmother gave him a fish.

   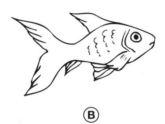   

Ⓐ   Ⓑ   Ⓒ

Find the sentence that matches the picture.

2   Mrs. Howard works hard.
   She brings the mail.

Ⓕ   Ⓖ   Ⓗ

Do this one the same way.

3

Ⓐ Two friends are having dinner.

Ⓑ The people are sitting around a table.

Ⓒ The class is studying spelling.

Directions: Read or listen to the story. Answer the questions about the story.

Kanisha was walking to her friend's house when it started to rain. She ran into a store to wait until it stopped.

The owner of the store said hello. His name was Mr. Minh.

It stopped raining in a few minutes. Kanisha left the store and started walking. She met her friend, Marty. They walked the rest of the way to his house.

4   Where was Kanisha going?

Ⓕ To school

Ⓖ To Marty's house

Ⓗ To the store

5   Who said hello?

Ⓐ Mr. Minh

Ⓑ Kanisha

Ⓒ Marty

6   Why did Kanisha run into the store?

Ⓕ She wanted to buy something.

Ⓖ It started to rain.

Ⓗ Marty was in the store.

7   How long did it rain?

Ⓐ For a minute

Ⓑ For a long time

Ⓒ For a few minutes

GO

Directions: Read or listen to the story. Choose the best answers to the questions about the story.

Elephants

Elephants can talk to each other. They do not use words like we use. They move their big floppy ears. They raise their long trunks in the air and wave them about. Elephants talk by moving their bodies. They can also make noises. One loud sound is called trumpeting. Elephants lift their trunks in the air when they make this sound. They sometimes make grunting sounds. Mothers seem to talk to their children with these noises. We do not understand what the elephants are saying. Scientists are trying to learn what elephants are saying.

8   How do elephants talk?

(F) With words

(G) With noises and grunts

(H) By running and jumping

9   When elephants trumpet, they

(A) lift their trunks in the air.

(B) stomp their feet on the ground.

(C) move from side to side.

10   Elephants do not

(F) lift their trunks.

(G) move their ears.

(H) use words.

To the Student:

These tests will give you a chance to put the tips you have learned to work.

A few last reminders . . .

- Be sure you understand all the directions before you begin each test. You may ask the teacher questions about the directions if you do not understand them.
- Work as quickly as you can during each test.
- When you change an answer, be sure to erase your first mark completely.

- You can guess at an answer or skip difficult items and go back to them later.
- Use the tips you have learned whenever you can.
- It is OK to be a little nervous. You may even do better.

Now that you have completed the lessons in this unit, you are on your way to scoring high!

STUDENT'S NAME			SCHOOL
LAST	FIRST	MI	TEACHER

FEMALE ○   MALE ○

BIRTH DATE

MONTH	DAY	YEAR
JAN ○	⓪ ⓪	⓪
FEB ○	① ①	①
MAR ○	② ②	②
APR ○	③ ③	③
MAY ○	④	④
JUN ○	⑤	⑤ ⑤
JUL ○	⑥	⑥ ⑥
AUG ○	⑦	⑦ ⑦
SEP ○	⑧	⑧ ⑧
OCT ○	⑨	⑨ ⑨
NOV ○		
DEC ○		

GRADE

Ⓚ ① ②

(Student name grid: columns of bubbles A through Z for Last, First, and MI)

PART 1   WORD ANALYSIS

EA Ⓐ Ⓑ Ⓒ Ⓓ	4 Ⓕ Ⓖ Ⓗ Ⓙ	11 Ⓐ Ⓑ Ⓒ Ⓓ	18 Ⓕ Ⓖ Ⓗ Ⓙ
EB Ⓕ Ⓖ Ⓗ Ⓙ	5 Ⓐ Ⓑ Ⓒ Ⓓ	12 Ⓕ Ⓖ Ⓗ Ⓙ	19 Ⓐ Ⓑ Ⓒ Ⓓ
EC Ⓐ Ⓑ Ⓒ Ⓓ	6 Ⓕ Ⓖ Ⓗ Ⓙ	13 Ⓐ Ⓑ Ⓒ Ⓓ	20 Ⓕ Ⓖ Ⓗ Ⓙ
ED Ⓕ Ⓖ Ⓗ Ⓙ	7 Ⓐ Ⓑ Ⓒ Ⓓ	14 Ⓕ Ⓖ Ⓗ Ⓙ	21 Ⓐ Ⓑ Ⓒ Ⓓ
1 Ⓐ Ⓑ Ⓒ Ⓓ	8 Ⓕ Ⓖ Ⓗ Ⓙ	15 Ⓐ Ⓑ Ⓒ Ⓓ	22 Ⓕ Ⓖ Ⓗ Ⓙ
2 Ⓕ Ⓖ Ⓗ Ⓙ	9 Ⓐ Ⓑ Ⓒ Ⓓ	16 Ⓕ Ⓖ Ⓗ Ⓙ	23 Ⓐ Ⓑ Ⓒ Ⓓ
3 Ⓐ Ⓑ Ⓒ Ⓓ	10 Ⓕ Ⓖ Ⓗ Ⓙ	17 Ⓐ Ⓑ Ⓒ Ⓓ	24 Ⓕ Ⓖ Ⓗ Ⓙ

PART 2   VOCABULARY

EA Ⓐ Ⓑ Ⓒ Ⓓ	5 Ⓐ Ⓑ Ⓒ Ⓓ	11 Ⓐ Ⓑ Ⓒ Ⓓ	17 Ⓐ Ⓑ Ⓒ Ⓓ	23 Ⓐ Ⓑ Ⓒ Ⓓ	29 Ⓐ Ⓑ Ⓒ Ⓓ
EB Ⓕ Ⓖ Ⓗ Ⓙ	6 Ⓕ Ⓖ Ⓗ Ⓙ	12 Ⓕ Ⓖ Ⓗ Ⓙ	18 Ⓕ Ⓖ Ⓗ Ⓙ	24 Ⓕ Ⓖ Ⓗ Ⓙ	30 Ⓕ Ⓖ Ⓗ Ⓙ
1 Ⓐ Ⓑ Ⓒ Ⓓ	7 Ⓐ Ⓑ Ⓒ Ⓓ	13 Ⓐ Ⓑ Ⓒ Ⓓ	19 Ⓐ Ⓑ Ⓒ Ⓓ	25 Ⓐ Ⓑ Ⓒ Ⓓ	31 Ⓐ Ⓑ Ⓒ Ⓓ
2 Ⓕ Ⓖ Ⓗ Ⓙ	8 Ⓕ Ⓖ Ⓗ Ⓙ	14 Ⓕ Ⓖ Ⓗ Ⓙ	20 Ⓕ Ⓖ Ⓗ Ⓙ	26 Ⓕ Ⓖ Ⓗ Ⓙ	
3 Ⓐ Ⓑ Ⓒ Ⓓ	9 Ⓐ Ⓑ Ⓒ Ⓓ	15 Ⓐ Ⓑ Ⓒ Ⓓ	21 Ⓐ Ⓑ Ⓒ Ⓓ	27 Ⓐ Ⓑ Ⓒ Ⓓ	
4 Ⓕ Ⓖ Ⓗ Ⓙ	10 Ⓕ Ⓖ Ⓗ Ⓙ	16 Ⓕ Ⓖ Ⓗ Ⓙ	22 Ⓕ Ⓖ Ⓗ Ⓙ	28 Ⓕ Ⓖ Ⓗ Ⓙ	

PART 3   READING COMPREHENSION

EA Ⓐ Ⓑ Ⓒ Ⓓ	2 Ⓕ Ⓖ Ⓗ Ⓙ	8 Ⓕ Ⓖ Ⓗ Ⓙ	14 Ⓕ Ⓖ Ⓗ Ⓙ	20 Ⓕ Ⓖ Ⓗ Ⓙ	26 Ⓕ Ⓖ Ⓗ Ⓙ
EB Ⓕ Ⓖ Ⓗ Ⓙ	3 Ⓐ Ⓑ Ⓒ Ⓓ	9 Ⓐ Ⓑ Ⓒ Ⓓ	15 Ⓐ Ⓑ Ⓒ Ⓓ	21 Ⓐ Ⓑ Ⓒ Ⓓ	27 Ⓐ Ⓑ Ⓒ Ⓓ
EC Ⓐ Ⓑ Ⓒ Ⓓ	4 Ⓕ Ⓖ Ⓗ Ⓙ	10 Ⓕ Ⓖ Ⓗ Ⓙ	16 Ⓕ Ⓖ Ⓗ Ⓙ	22 Ⓕ Ⓖ Ⓗ Ⓙ	28 Ⓕ Ⓖ Ⓗ Ⓙ
ED Ⓕ Ⓖ Ⓗ Ⓙ	5 Ⓐ Ⓑ Ⓒ Ⓓ	11 Ⓐ Ⓑ Ⓒ Ⓓ	17 Ⓐ Ⓑ Ⓒ Ⓓ	23 Ⓐ Ⓑ Ⓒ Ⓓ	29 Ⓐ Ⓑ Ⓒ Ⓓ
EE Ⓐ Ⓑ Ⓒ Ⓓ	6 Ⓕ Ⓖ Ⓗ Ⓙ	12 Ⓕ Ⓖ Ⓗ Ⓙ	18 Ⓕ Ⓖ Ⓗ Ⓙ	24 Ⓕ Ⓖ Ⓗ Ⓙ	
1 Ⓐ Ⓑ Ⓒ Ⓓ	7 Ⓐ Ⓑ Ⓒ Ⓓ	13 Ⓐ Ⓑ Ⓒ Ⓓ	19 Ⓐ Ⓑ Ⓒ Ⓓ	25 Ⓐ Ⓑ Ⓒ Ⓓ	

Part 1 Word Analysis

Example A

Directions: Choose the best answer to the questions. The first one has been done for you. Do numbers 1-6 the same way.

Which letter does the word "egg" begin with?

e	a	i	u
Ⓐ	Ⓑ	Ⓒ	Ⓓ

Which letter does the word "sock" begin with?

e	x	a	s
Ⓐ	Ⓑ	Ⓒ	Ⓓ

1

Which letter does the word "dog" begin with?

d	l	t	b
Ⓕ	Ⓖ	Ⓗ	Ⓙ

2

Which letter does the word "apple" begin with?

s	o	e	a
Ⓐ	Ⓑ	Ⓒ	Ⓓ

3

Which letter does the word "teddy bear" begin with?

d	p	t	g
Ⓕ	Ⓖ	Ⓗ	Ⓙ

4

Which letter does the word "jet" begin with?

q	j	l	i
Ⓐ	Ⓑ	Ⓒ	Ⓓ

5

Which letter does the word "fold" begin with?

k	f	s	c
Ⓕ	Ⓖ	Ⓗ	Ⓙ

6

STOP

Example B   **Directions:** Choose the best answer to the questions.
The first one has been done for you. Practice on the second one.

Which picture has the same beginning sound as "face"?

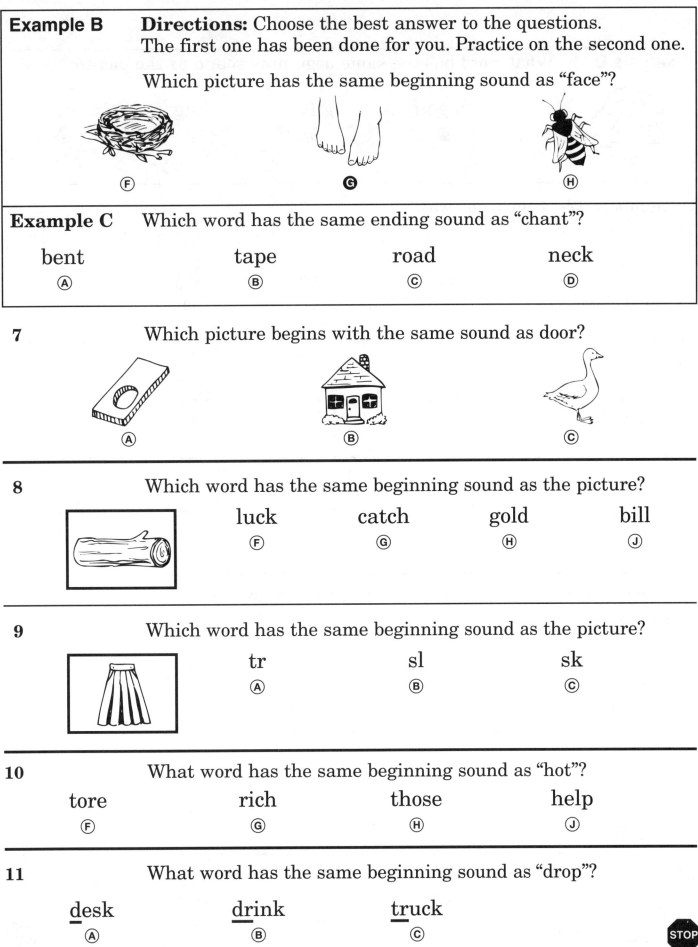

Ⓕ   Ⓖ   Ⓗ

Example C   Which word has the same ending sound as "chant"?

bent   tape   road   neck
Ⓐ   Ⓑ   Ⓒ   Ⓓ

7   Which picture begins with the same sound as door?

Ⓐ   Ⓑ   Ⓒ

8   Which word has the same beginning sound as the picture?

luck   catch   gold   bill
Ⓕ   Ⓖ   Ⓗ   Ⓙ

9   Which word has the same beginning sound as the picture?

tr   sl   sk
Ⓐ   Ⓑ   Ⓒ

10   What word has the same beginning sound as "hot"?

tore   rich   those   help
Ⓕ   Ⓖ   Ⓗ   Ⓙ

11   What word has the same beginning sound as "drop"?

desk   drink   truck
Ⓐ   Ⓑ   Ⓒ

STOP

Example D   What word has the same beginning sound as the picture?

wagon   gift   bag   lip
F   G   H   J

Do numbers 12-14 the same way.

12

ride   nice   play   slow
F   G   H   J

13

throw   grow   jump   leaf
A   B   C   D

14

call   read   yes   black
F   G   H   J

What word has the same ending sound as the picture?
Do numbers 15-17 the same way.

15

first   most   hurt   wood
A   B   C   D

16

kind   fork   pool   sit
F   G   H   J

17

many   post   branch   rope
A   B   C   D

STOP

Which picture has the same beginning sound as "fall"?

18   Ⓕ   Ⓖ   Ⓗ

Which picture begins with the same sound as "stamp"?

 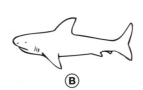 

19   Ⓐ   Ⓑ   Ⓒ

Which word begins with the same sound as "young"?

judge   yellow   pound

20   Ⓕ   Ⓖ   Ⓗ

Which word begins with the same sound as "smile"?

empty   smell   real

21   Ⓐ   Ⓑ   Ⓒ

Which word begins with the same sound as "desk"?

dark   best   lock

22   Ⓕ   Ⓖ   Ⓗ

Which picture rhymes with "rent"?

   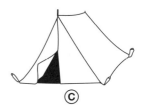

23   Ⓐ   Ⓑ   Ⓒ

Which picture rhymes with "box"?

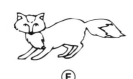   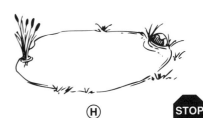

24   Ⓕ   Ⓖ   Ⓗ   STOP

Example A   **Directions:** Choose the picture or the word that matches the words. The first one has been done for you. Do numbers 1-6 the same way.

Something that is burning

(A)   (B)   (C)

1   Something you listen to

(A)   (B)   (C)

2   Something messy

(F)   (G)   (H)

3   A farm animal

(A)   (B)   (C)

4   To take it easy

rest	work	run	lift
(F)	(G)	(H)	(J)

5   A part of your body

shoe	floor	arm	person
(A)	(B)	(C)	(D)

6   A place you buy food

ocean	street	bank	market
(F)	(G)	(H)	(J)

STOP

Directions: Look at the picture. What word in each group matches the picture?

Example B This one has been done for you.

reach	fox	prince
Ⓕ	**Ⓖ**	Ⓗ

Example C Practice on this one.

chicken	later	piece
Ⓐ	Ⓑ	Ⓒ

Do numbers 1-18 the same way.

7
woman	unless	strange
Ⓐ	Ⓑ	Ⓒ

8
find	car	open
Ⓕ	Ⓖ	Ⓗ

9
trick	roof	window
Ⓐ	Ⓑ	Ⓒ

13
month	break	monkey
Ⓐ	Ⓑ	Ⓒ

14
chain	climb	list
Ⓕ	Ⓖ	Ⓗ

15
tree	ground	pool
Ⓐ	Ⓑ	Ⓒ

10
field	pond	forest
Ⓕ	Ⓖ	Ⓗ

11
frog	reason	frost
Ⓐ	Ⓑ	Ⓒ

12
watch	them	swim
Ⓕ	Ⓖ	Ⓗ

16
tape	rope	roll
Ⓕ	Ⓖ	Ⓗ

17
king	choice	knot
Ⓐ	Ⓑ	Ⓒ

18
tie	let	pin
Ⓕ	Ⓖ	Ⓗ

STOP

Directions: Read the sentences. Choose the picture that matches the sentence.

Sally read a newspaper.

   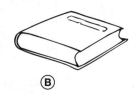   

19   Ⓐ   Ⓑ   Ⓒ

Do this one the same way.

The horse stood on top of the hill.

20   Ⓕ   Ⓖ   Ⓗ

Find the word that will complete the sentence.

I ate an _____ for lunch.

early   apple   usual   also

21   Ⓐ   Ⓑ   Ⓒ   Ⓓ

Do numbers 22 and 23 the same way.

Lou walked to the _____ .

quickly   down   over   park

22   Ⓕ   Ⓖ   Ⓗ   Ⓙ

Sandy was _____ after the game.

soon   later   tired   sat

23   Ⓐ   Ⓑ   Ⓒ   Ⓓ

STOP

What word means the same as the underlined word? Do numbers 24-27 the same way.

24 Did you <u>clean</u> the window?

Ⓕ close

Ⓖ wash

Ⓗ open

Ⓙ fix

25 That is a <u>silly</u> idea.

Ⓐ good

Ⓑ wonderful

Ⓒ foolish

Ⓓ strange

26 It is <u>almost</u> time to go.

Ⓕ nearly

Ⓖ exactly

Ⓗ not

Ⓙ now

27 The car stopped <u>suddenly</u>.

Ⓐ slowly

Ⓑ there

Ⓒ nearby

Ⓓ quickly

What word means the opposite of the underlined word? Do numbers 28-31 the same way.

28 Heavy things will often <u>float</u>.

Ⓕ roll

Ⓖ fall

Ⓗ drop

Ⓙ sink

29 She <u>forgot</u> her pen.

Ⓐ lost

Ⓑ remembered

Ⓒ brought

Ⓓ used

30 My room is really <u>messy</u>.

Ⓕ large

Ⓖ small

Ⓗ neat

Ⓙ nice

31 The river is <u>high</u> today.

Ⓐ low

Ⓑ cold

Ⓒ icy

Ⓓ loud

STOP

Example A   **Directions:** Read or listen to the story. Then choose the best answer to the question. This one has been done for you.

It was afternoon on the farm. The horse was running through the field. And the cow was lying down.

Which picture shows what the cow was doing?

Ⓐ   Ⓑ   Ⓒ

Do this one the same way.

1 Katie has a cat named Zack. Zack likes to run around and play. He likes to climb on furniture. When he is all done, he sleeps in his favorite place—under the table. Where does Zack sleep?

   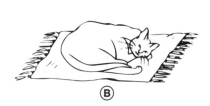   

Ⓐ   Ⓑ   Ⓒ

Read the sentences. Match the sentence to the picture.

2 Nina went to the pet store. She bought a fish.

Ⓕ   Ⓖ   Ⓗ

Look at the picture. Match the picture to the right sentence.

3

Ⓐ They had a good time at the beach.

Ⓑ Beth's parents went shopping.

Ⓒ Marla and Donald will get married.

STOP

Example B Look at the picture. Match the picture to the right sentence. This one has been done for you. Do numbers 4-8 the same way.

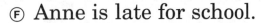

- Ⓕ Anne is late for school.
- Ⓖ The weather is nice today.
- Ⓗ The library is closed.

4

- Ⓕ The children are hungry.
- Ⓖ Deanna likes to cook.
- Ⓗ Did Deanna do her homework?

5

- Ⓐ Mrs. Rayburn is watching the news.
- Ⓑ Mrs. Rayburn is taking a nap.
- Ⓒ The television is new.

6

- Ⓕ The frog is swimming.
- Ⓖ Fish are in the pond.
- Ⓗ The frog is by the pond.

7

- Ⓐ The pond is small.
- Ⓑ Tonya saved her friends.
- Ⓒ Children like to play.

8

- Ⓕ The floor is clean.
- Ⓖ Bobby is in his chair.
- Ⓗ Bobby lost his watch.

Directions: Read the sentence. Match the sentence to the picture.

Example C This one has been done for you.

You can open this.
It lets you into a garden.

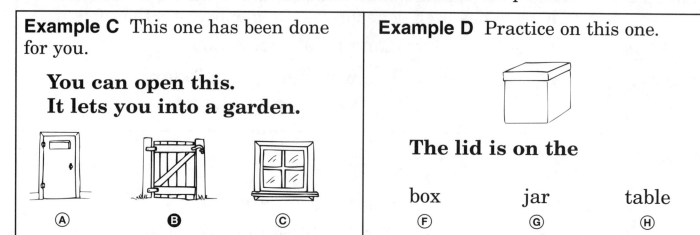

Ⓐ   **Ⓑ**   Ⓒ

Example D Practice on this one.

The lid is on the

box   jar   table
Ⓕ   Ⓖ   Ⓗ

Do numbers 9-13 the same way.

9 You can look through it.
You can see very far.

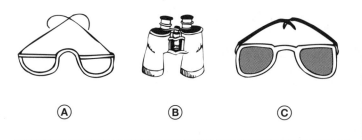

Ⓐ   Ⓑ   Ⓒ

10 She is talking to her friend.
Her friend is far away.

Ⓕ   Ⓖ   Ⓗ

11 The girl is

walking   standing   sitting
Ⓐ   Ⓑ   Ⓒ

12 She is

mixing   baking   carrying
Ⓕ   Ⓖ   Ⓗ

13 something in a

pot   bowl   dish
Ⓐ   Ⓑ   Ⓒ

STOP

Example E   **Directions:** Read or listen to the story. Then choose the best answers to the questions. The first one has been done for you.

Trudy is in the car.

Mrs. Wilson is driving.

Lincoln is waiting for them.

Who is waiting?

Ⓐ Trudy

🅑 Lincoln

Ⓒ Mrs. Wilson

Do numbers 14-17 the same way.

Mr. Renzulli likes to garden.

He is planting flowers now.

His neighbor, Julius, will help Mr. Renzulli pull weeds.

Later in the spring, he will plant vegetables.

Mr. Renzulli will share the vegetables with his friends.

14 What is Mr. Renzulli planting now?

Ⓕ Flowers

Ⓖ Vegetables

Ⓗ Weeds

15 What is this story mostly about?

Ⓐ Flowers

Ⓑ Friends

Ⓒ Gardening

16 Who is Julius?

Ⓕ Mr. Renzulli's son

Ⓖ Mr. Renzulli's neighbor

Ⓗ Mr. Renzulli's nephew

17 What will Mr. Renzulli do with the vegetables?

Ⓐ Sell them to his friends and neighbors

Ⓑ Let the birds eat them

Ⓒ Share them with his friends

GO

Directions: Read or listen to the story. Choose the best answers to the questions about the story.

Tom's New Home

"You have too many cats, Amy," her mother said. "You must find new homes for some of them." Amy was sad but she knew her mother was right.

One day, Amy's aunt came to visit. "I will take a cat home with me," she said. "I would like to have a cat."

Amy caught Tom, her newest cat, and put him in a box. Tom did not like being carried to the car. He cried, "Meow. Meow." Amy put the box in the car, then placed a bowl of water and some cat food in the box.

Aunt Patricia drove Tom to her home. When she opened the box, Tom was afraid. He ran under the bed. Aunt Patricia tried to catch him.

Tom was even more afraid than he had been before. He ran and ran. Amy's aunt decided to wait. She held some cat treats in her hand and spoke softly. Tom came up to her and ate the treats. Then he jumped on her lap. Tom had a new home. Aunt Patricia had a new friend.

18 Tom was a

   ⓕ dog.

   ⓖ bird.

   ⓗ cat.

19 Amy did not want to

   Ⓐ keep all her cats.

   Ⓑ give her cats away.

   Ⓒ visit with Aunt Patricia.

20 At first, Tom felt

   ⓕ happy.

   ⓖ afraid.

   ⓗ sad.

21 In the future,

   Ⓐ Tom will be happy.

   Ⓑ Aunt Patricia will move.

   Ⓒ Amy will have no pets.

GO

Directions: Read or listen to the story. Choose the best answers to the questions about the story.

The plane landed at the airport. When the people got off, John saw his grandmother. He ran up to her and gave her a hug.

John, his father and mother, and his grandmother got the bags. Then they took the elevator to the parking lot.

In the car, John told his grandmother he had a surprise for her at home. It had four legs, a tail, and a wet nose.

---

22 How did John feel when he saw his grandmother?

Ⓕ Happy

Ⓖ Surprised

Ⓗ Sad

23 What did John and his family do after his grandmother arrived?

Ⓐ Went to the car

Ⓑ Went home

Ⓒ Got the bags

24 How did everyone get to the parking lot?

Ⓕ By car

Ⓖ By elevator

Ⓗ By walking

25 What was John's surprise?

Ⓐ A puppy

Ⓑ Flowers

Ⓒ A new house

STOP

Directions: Read or listen to the story. Choose the best answers to the questions about the story.

Who was the best monkey?

All the monkeys in the forest were excited. This was the day the leader of the monkeys was chosen. It was a very important day for all the monkeys. It came only once a year.

By noon, all of the monkeys had gathered near a special tree. The old King of the Monkeys was named Butu. He would help to choose the new leader.

Many monkeys wanted to be king. They climbed up and down the special tree very quickly. They jumped from branch to branch. The monkey that did the best tricks would be chosen king.

One monkey climbed and jumped better than all the others. Butu decided this monkey would be king. When the monkey climbed to the top of the tree to receive the crown, everyone was surprised. This monkey was a girl named Chota, but girls could not be king!

Butu thought very hard about this problem. Chota was the best climber and jumper, but she was a girl. Then Butu had an idea. He said, "Chota is the best climber and jumper, but she cannot be king. So this year, we will have a queen instead." He gave Chota the crown and all the other monkeys cheered.

26 In this story, Butu was

  (F) wise.

  (G) angry.

  (H) sad.

  (J) foolish.

28 This story is

  (F) true.

  (G) make-believe.

  (H) about people.

  (J) about trees.

27 Before Chota, the monkeys

  (A) always had a queen.

  (B) never had a leader.

  (C) lived on the ground.

  (D) always had a king.

29 Which words in the story tell where the leader of the monkeys was chosen?

  (A) "...once a year."

  (B) "...chosen king."

  (C) "...very quickly."

  (D) "...a special tree."

STOP

Table of Contents
Language

Lesson 1 · Listening Skills

Example

Directions: Read or listen to each story. Then choose the best answer to the question. The first one has been done for you. Do numbers 1-7 the same way.

A Mrs. Hopkins runs a store. She sells things that people use in an office or in school. What things does Mrs. Hopkins sell in her store?

Ⓐ

Ⓑ

Ⓒ

 **Listen carefully to or read the story and look at all the pictures.**

Practice

1 Mr. Jones and his family went to the park for a picnic. They brought salad and chicken and a ball to play with. They forgot one thing—dessert! What did Mr. Jones forget?

Ⓐ

Ⓑ

Ⓒ

2 Pat's grandmother made her something to wear outside. It wasn't a hat. What did Pat look like when she went outside?

Ⓕ

Ⓖ

Ⓗ

3 Rob drew a picture in the sand with a stick. He drew a square and a circle inside a square. Then Nina came by and drew two more circles inside the square. What did Rob's drawing look like after Nina drew her circles?

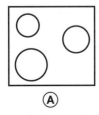
Ⓐ

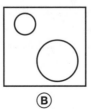
Ⓑ

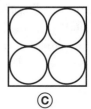
Ⓒ

GO ⟩

4 Nate was sitting at the table. He looked at something on the table and said, "It's almost time for supper." What did Nate find on the table?

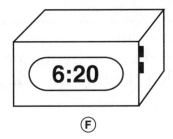

Ⓕ

Ⓖ

Ⓗ

---

5 Marco was walking to school one day. He saw a set of keys and bent over to pick them up. What picture shows Marco on his way to school?

Ⓐ

Ⓑ

Ⓒ

---

6 Allie and her mom went to a yard sale. They bought something that Allie could use for her science fair project. What did Allie buy at the yard sale?

Ⓕ

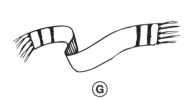

Ⓖ

Ⓗ

---

7 Dale was playing a board game. He had to make the word "yesterday" out of the letters. What letters did Dale have?

EST   ERD   **YES   DAY**   **STE   RDA**

Ⓐ   Ⓑ   Ⓒ

STOP

Examples   **Directions:** Read or listen to each story. Then choose the best answers to the questions.

B The sun is a star. It is much closer to the earth than other stars. The earth moves around the sun. The sun is a _____.
The first one has been done for you.

(F) cold

(G) a star

(H) tiny

C Practice on this one.
Margo walked into the living room. Everyone yelled "Happy Birthday!" Margo felt so _____.

(A) sad

(B) tired

(C) surprised

8 Ringo was walking to school. He found some bottles and he threw them out in a can. Ringo put the bottles _____.

(F) in a trash bag

(G) in a box

(H) in a trash can

9 Mary likes to build things. She made a bench to put in her room. She built a table. Mary likes to _____.

(A) build things

(B) play in the park

(C) cook

10 Where did Mary put the bench?

(F) in the kitchen

(G) in her room

(H) on a table

11 Lily found her brother in her room. She wanted to do her homework on the computer, but her brother was already playing on it! Who likes to play games on the computer?
Lily's _____.

(A) mother

(B) father

(C) brother

12 Raccoons are funny animals. They wash their food before eating. They also know how to open things— even doors. Some people have found raccoons in their kitchen! Raccoons like to _____.

(F) wash their food

(G) eat fruit

(H) play in trees

13 People have found raccoons _____.

(A) in the car

(B) in the basement

(C) in the kitchen

STOP

Example   **Directions:** Read or listen to each story. Then choose the best answer to the question. The first one has been done for you. Do numbers 1-7 the same way.

A   Bruce is going to Amber's house for a birthday party. What will he see at Amber's house?

Ⓐ

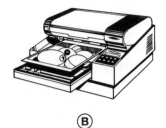
Ⓑ

Ⓒ

   **If you are not sure which answer is correct, take your best guess.**

Practice

1   Page wants to draw circles on a piece of paper. What will help her do that?

Ⓐ

Ⓑ

Ⓒ

---

2   The garden store is having a sale on plants in black pots. What is on sale at the garden store?

Ⓕ

Ⓖ

Ⓗ

---

3   Kirk is going on a camping trip. He is taking something to play with. What is he taking?

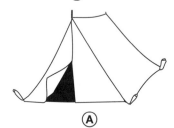
Ⓐ

Ⓑ

Ⓒ

GO ▷

4 Mae is going to her aunt's wedding. Which one is Mae?

Ⓕ

Ⓖ

Ⓗ

5 When Lamar cleaned his room he found lots of things he forgot he had. One was a toy that made noise when he blew in it. What did Lamar find?

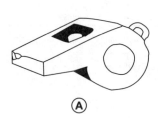
Ⓐ

Ⓑ

Ⓒ

6 Maureen found some feathers. She arranged them from the smallest to the largest. Which picture shows what Maureen did?

Ⓕ

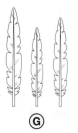
Ⓖ

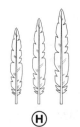
Ⓗ

7 Vern was getting ready for school. He washed his face. He got his drum ready for band practice. Then he noticed something he needed <u>two</u> of at school. What did Vern need two of?

Ⓐ

Ⓑ

Ⓒ

STOP

Example   **Directions:** Read or listen to the story. Choose the best answer to the question. The first one has been done for you. Do numbers 1-8 the same way.

E1 When Kelly's mother came home from work, she told her a funny story. After work, a storm came up. They only had one umbrella. Which picture shows what happened?

 Ⓐ
 Ⓑ
 Ⓒ

1 Ethan went on a plane ride with his aunt and uncle. When the plane took off, Ethan could see the park where he sometimes played. Which picture shows Ethan's plane taking off?

 Ⓐ
 Ⓑ
 Ⓒ

2 The teacher asked the students to name something round. They named the things that were round and one thing that was almost round. Which picture shows something that is almost round?

 Ⓕ
 Ⓖ
 Ⓗ

3 Travis reached into a drawer and found something long and thin. It wasn't for building things and it wasn't for eating soup. What was it?

 Ⓐ
 Ⓑ
 Ⓒ

4 Monica was washing the dishes when she noticed a spot on a pot. When she tried to rub it off, the spot ended up on her hand. Then she wiped the spot on a towel. Where was the spot when Monica first noticed it?

 Ⓕ
 Ⓖ
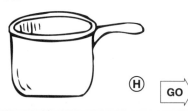 Ⓗ GO▷

5 Harold is playing with his train while he is waiting for his friend George. Then they will go to the store. Which picture shows Harold waiting for his friend?

Ⓐ

Ⓑ

Ⓒ

6 Pam is going on a vacation to the ocean. It will be warm there. What should Pam bring to help her swim in the ocean?

Ⓕ

Ⓖ

Ⓗ

7 Ms. Miller went shopping. First she bought groceries. Then she bought a present. Finally, she had pizza for lunch. What did Ms. Miller buy first?

Ⓐ

Ⓑ

Ⓒ

8 Some children are drawing animals. Art drew an animal with four legs that lives on a farm. Dot drew an animal that can fly and swim. Millie drew an animal that can swim. Which animal did Dot draw?

Ⓕ

Ⓖ

Ⓗ

STOP

Directions: Read or listen to the story. Choose the best answer to the question. Do numbers 9-14 the same way.

This one has been done for you.

E2 Rob was late to school. He ran out the door and down the street. The bus driver smiled at him. Where was Rob going?

(F) home

(G) **to school**

(H) to the store

Practice on this one.

E3 Alaska is the largest state. It is far away from the other states. It is closer to Russia than it is to the United States. In fact, Alaska was once part of Russia.
What country was Alaska once part of?

(A) part of Russia

(B) part of Canada

(C) part of England

---

9 Janet and her mother went to the store to buy a gift for Janet's aunt. Janet saw a friend. Then she had a snack. Why did Janet go to the store?

(A) see a friend

(B) buy a gift

(C) have a snack

10 Tony's grandmother has a new plant. It's from Egypt. It's a papyrus. Where is the papyrus plant from?

(F) Japan

(G) Italy

(H) Egypt

11 Tony's grandma told Tony that the plant was used to make a kind of paper. What was papyrus used to make?

(A) shoe

(B) paper

(C) pot

12 Trees are amazing plants. Their roots protect the soil. Their leaves make oxygen. The roots of a tree

(F) protect the soil

(G) make oxygen

(H) make wood

13 Trudy was sneezing. Her nose was running. Her mom made her stay home from school. Trudy stayed home because she

(A) stayed up late

(B) had a cold

(C) hurt her foot

14 Trudy didn't feel well enough to eat. She slept all day. What did Trudy eat?

(F) toast

(G) soup

(H) nothing

STOP

NUMBER RIGHT _____

Lesson 4 Capitalization

Examples **Directions:** Look at the sentence. Look at each part of the sentence. Is there a word that needs a capital letter? Choose the part of the sentence that needs a capital letter. If none of the words should be capitalized, choose None.

This one has been done for you.		
A Call me	on wednesday.	None
Ⓐ	●	Ⓒ
Practice on this one.		
B Don't drop	your glass.	None
Ⓕ	Ⓖ	Ⓗ

 **Tips** **Sentences begin with capital letters. Important words in a sentence begin with capital letters.**

Do numbers 1-5 the same way.

Practice

1 This is | jim's coat. | None
  Ⓐ | Ⓑ | Ⓒ

2 Can i | have some water. | None
  Ⓕ | Ⓖ | Ⓗ

3 In July | we will swim. | None
  Ⓐ | Ⓑ | Ⓒ

4 Her party | is on thursday. | None
  Ⓕ | Ⓖ | Ⓗ

5 tell her | the joke. | None
  Ⓐ | Ⓑ | Ⓒ

STOP

Examples

Directions: Read or listen to the story. Choose the best answer to the question. Do numbers 6 and 7 the same way.

Directions: Read or listen to each question. Choose the best answer to the question. Do numbers 8-11 the same way.

C Rusty is writing a letter to his aunt about his new friend. Look at the underlined part. How should Rusty have written the underlined part?

I have a new friend.
Her name is Lucy Smith.
<u>   (1)   </u>

Ⓐ lucy smith

Ⓑ lucy Smith

Ⓒ The way he did

D In the sentence, "When can i play ball?", which letter should be a capital letter?

Ⓕ can

Ⓖ i

Ⓗ play

E In the sentence, "Tell nora lunch is ready," which word should begin with a capital letter?

Ⓐ nora

Ⓑ lunch

Ⓒ ready

To The Beach

My family went on vacation. We left on <u>Friday, June 4.</u>
<u>   (1)   </u>

We drove to <u>North carolina.</u> It was wonderful.
<u>   (2)   </u>

6 Linda wrote an essay about her summer vacation. How should she have written the date (1)?

Ⓕ Friday, june 4

Ⓖ friday, june 4

Ⓗ The way she did

7 How should Linda have written the name of the place she and her family visited (2)?

Ⓐ north carolina

Ⓑ North Carolina

Ⓒ The way she did

---

8 The store is closed on saturday.

Ⓕ store

Ⓖ closed

Ⓗ saturday

9 where did you see the bear?

Ⓐ where

Ⓑ see

Ⓒ bear

10 Did rose make the bird house?

Ⓕ rose

Ⓖ make

Ⓗ house

11 We had lunch in denver.

Ⓐ had

Ⓑ lunch

Ⓒ denver

Examples   **Directions:** These sentences may need punctuation at the end. Choose the right punctuation mark for each sentence. If no punctuation is needed, mark None.

A   This one has been done for you.
   She is nice
   Ⓐ ?   ● .   Ⓒ None

B   Practice on this one. Then do numbers 1-5 the same way.
   How old is your dog?
   Ⓕ .   Ⓖ !   Ⓗ None

 **Look for missing punctuation at the end of the sentence.**

Practice

1 That is my book
   Ⓐ .   Ⓑ !   Ⓒ None

2 Did you call me
   Ⓕ !   Ⓖ ?   Ⓗ None

3 Are we there yet?
   Ⓐ !   Ⓑ .   Ⓒ None

4 The door is open
   Ⓕ ?   Ⓖ .   Ⓗ None

5 Bill is late
   Ⓐ .   Ⓑ !   Ⓒ None

STOP

Directions: Look at the underlined sentence. Does it need punctuation? Choose the correct punctuation.

Examples

> This one has been done for you.
> C *It is cold today*
>   (1)
>
> *I will wear a coat.*
>
> Ⓐ today?
> ❸ today.
> Ⓒ today!
>
> Do numbers 6 and 7 the same way.

Directions: Look at each sentence and answer the questions.

> D That is an apple tree
>   What punctuation mark should come after tree? This one has been done for you.
>
> ❺ tree.
> Ⓖ tree!
> Ⓗ tree?
>
> E Where is Steve
>   What punctuation mark should come after Steve? Practice on this one.
>
> Ⓐ Steve.
> Ⓑ Steve!
> Ⓒ Steve?
>
> Do numbers 8-11 the same way.

A Surprise

Mandy heard a funny sound. <u>What could it be</u>
                                    (1)

She <u>didn't</u> know what it was. Mandy asked her mother.
     (2)

6 Ⓕ be?
    Ⓖ be.
    Ⓗ be!

7 Ⓐ did'nt
    Ⓑ didnt'
    Ⓒ The way it is

8 Quick, come with me
    Ⓕ me.
    Ⓖ me!
    Ⓗ me?

9 How much is that book
    Ⓐ book?
    Ⓑ book.
    Ⓒ book!

10 Kamisha swam in the lake
    Ⓕ lake!
    Ⓖ lake?
    Ⓗ lake.

11 The sun is shining
    Ⓐ shining?
    Ⓑ shining.
    Ⓒ shining!

STOP

Examples   **Directions:** Choose the sentence that uses correct capitalization and punctuation.

This one has been done for you.	Practice on this one.

A   Ⓐ   Today is Tuesday
     🅑   I am in school.
     Ⓒ   where are you?
	B Ⓕ This soup is good.
	     Ⓖ Are you hungry
	     Ⓗ pass me the bread

Remember, find the answer that has correct capitalization and punctuation.

Do numbers 1-6 the same way.

Practice

1   Ⓐ   i take long walks.
    Ⓑ   Swimming is fun
    Ⓒ   Can you run fast?

4   Ⓕ   The plane is large
    Ⓖ   My mother took a trip.
    Ⓗ   We will meet her?

2   Ⓕ   School is closed on Friday.
    Ⓖ   The game is on saturday
    Ⓗ   will you visit on Sunday?

5   Ⓐ   Where is richard.
    Ⓑ   Can you hear Ken.
    Ⓒ   Did you call Donna?

3   Ⓐ   Give Mark this ball?
    Ⓑ   How tall is Sue?
    Ⓒ   Can you reach the switch

6   Ⓕ   That bird is beautiful.
    Ⓖ   The tree in your yard is tall
    Ⓗ   can you hear the bird?

STOP

Examples   **Directions:** Which part of each sentence needs a capital letter? If neither part needs a capital letter, mark None.

This one has been done for you.

E1   Let judy | come with us.   None
       Ⓐ   Ⓑ   Ⓒ

Practice on this one.

E2   My birthday | is in March.   None
       Ⓕ   Ⓖ   Ⓗ

Do numbers 1-6 the same way.

1   We named | our dog andy.   None
      Ⓐ   Ⓑ   Ⓒ

2   When can | i help?   None
      Ⓕ   Ⓖ   Ⓗ

3   My friend | went home.   None
      Ⓐ   Ⓑ   Ⓒ

4   can she | swim far?   None
      Ⓕ   Ⓖ   Ⓗ

5   I study | every night.   None
      Ⓐ   Ⓑ   Ⓒ

6   On friday | we went shopping.   None
      Ⓕ   Ⓖ   Ⓗ

STOP

73

Directions: Read or listen to the story. Choose the best answer to the question. The first one has been done for you. Do numbers 6 and 7 the same way.

Directions: Look at each sentence. Mark the word that should begin with a capital letter. The first one has been done for you. Do the next one for practice. Then do numbers 9-12 the same way.

E3   Robbie wrote a letter to his friend about his sister. Look at the underlined part. How should he have written the underlined part?

Vera is my sister.
Her birthday is on Fri Day.
                          (1)

Ⓐ   friday
🅑   Friday
Ⓒ   The way he did

E4   some socks are on the table.

Ⓕ   some
Ⓖ   socks
Ⓗ   table

E5   Is this where fred lives?

Ⓐ   this
Ⓑ   fred
Ⓒ   lives

A Surprise

mandy's mother smiled. It is a kitten.
_____
     (1)
He is in the box in the kitchen. His name is Andrew.
                                              (2)

7   Jesse wrote a short story for her class. In her story, how should she have written the first underlined part?
Ⓐ   Mandy's mother
Ⓑ   Mandy's Mother
Ⓒ   The way it is

8   How should she have written the kitten's name in the second underlined part?
Ⓕ   andrew
Ⓖ   An Drew
Ⓗ   The way it is

9   the water is deep
Ⓐ   the
Ⓑ   water
Ⓒ   deep

10   The story is by john Maiden.
Ⓕ   story
Ⓖ   is
Ⓗ   john

11   We will arrive on monday night.
Ⓐ   will
Ⓑ   monday
Ⓒ   night

12   Can i go to the store?
Ⓕ   i
Ⓖ   go
Ⓗ   store

STOP

Directions: Look at the sentence. Does it need punctuation at the end? Choose the correct punctuation. If the sentence does not need punctuation, choose None.

The first one has been done for you. Do the next one for practice. Then do numbers 13-18 the same way.

E6 My house is on this street.

Ⓕ ?   Ⓖ !   ● None

E7 Jump out of the way

Ⓐ ?   Ⓑ !   Ⓒ None

---

13 Where did you find it

Ⓐ .   Ⓑ ?   Ⓒ None

14 George rode his bike

Ⓕ !   Ⓖ .   Ⓗ None

15 Can we go to the park

Ⓐ ?   Ⓑ .   Ⓒ None

16 Don't touch that hot dish

Ⓕ !   Ⓖ .   Ⓗ None

17 The box is empty

Ⓐ ?   Ⓑ .   Ⓒ None

18 Who dropped this pen

Ⓕ .   Ⓖ ?   Ⓗ None

STOP

Directions: Look at the underlined sentence. Does it need punctuation at the end? Mark the correct answer. The first one has been done for you. Do numbers 19 and 20 the same way.

Directions: Look at these sentences. Should they have punctuation? The first one has been done for you. Do the next one for practice. Then do numbers 21-24 the same way.

E8   *What time is it*
              (1)

We should go home soon.

- ● it?
- Ⓖ it.
- Ⓗ it!

E9   Run over here

- Ⓐ here.
- Ⓑ here?
- ● here!

E10   The sun is hot

- Ⓕ hot!
- Ⓖ hot.
- Ⓗ hot?

A Surprise

Mandy hugged the kitten
                (1)
He purred for her.

Is he mine
     (2)
Her mother said the kitten was hers.

19   Ⓐ kitten!

      Ⓑ kitten.

      Ⓒ kitten?

20   Ⓕ mine?

      Ⓖ mine!

      Ⓗ mine.

21   The store is closed

      Ⓐ closed.

      Ⓑ closed!

      Ⓒ closed?

22   How many apples do you have

      Ⓕ have!

      Ⓖ have.

      Ⓗ have?

23   Watch out for the bee

      Ⓐ bee!

      Ⓑ bee?

      Ⓒ bee.

24   Please hand me a nail

      Ⓕ nail?

      Ⓖ nail.

      Ⓗ nail!

STOP

Directions: Choose the sentence that uses correct punctuation and capitalization. The first one has been done for you. Practice on the next one.

E11	Ⓐ	John and Sally are friends
	Ⓑ	we saw Carol and Lou.
	Ⓒ	Did Barb or Matt come?

E12	Ⓕ	i fell in the snow.
	Ⓖ	It was cold.
	Ⓗ	We had fun

Do numbers 25-32 the same way.

25 Ⓐ This is Ted's watch.
    Ⓑ Where is Carla's coat
    Ⓒ will Jane be there?

26 Ⓕ We saw her in july.
    Ⓖ April was warm
    Ⓗ How many days are there in August?

27 Ⓐ What day will you leave
    Ⓑ She met my Uncle Dan.
    Ⓒ our trip is next month.

28 Ⓕ Give Mark this ball?
    Ⓖ how tall is Sue?
    Ⓗ Is this seat taken?

29 Ⓐ on Tuesday we will play ball.
    Ⓑ Can you come on Wednesday?
    Ⓒ Meet me on friday.

30 Ⓕ Florida has many beaches.
    Ⓖ iowa has large farms.
    Ⓗ Have you visited Ohio.

31 Ⓐ Let's go fishing.
    Ⓑ Tim likes to draw?
    Ⓒ maxine runs often.

32 Ⓕ Is this dish clean
    Ⓖ use this towel.
    Ⓗ Turn the water off.

STOP

Lesson 8   Usage

Examples   **Directions:** Choose the word that completes the sentence.

This one has been done for you.	Practice on this one.
A Mark _____ the box.	**B** The light _____ .
Ⓐ carry	Ⓕ on the table
Ⓑ carrying	Ⓖ bright
⦿ carried	Ⓗ is on

 **Tips**   **Try each answer choice in the blank.**

Do numbers 1-6 the same way.

Practice

1   It is _____ today than yesterday.

  Ⓐ   cold

  Ⓑ   colder

  Ⓒ   coldest

2   _____ sat on the porch.

  Ⓕ   A dog

  Ⓖ   This morning

  Ⓗ   Barking

3   This is a _____ movie.

  Ⓐ   more shorter

  Ⓑ   shortest

  Ⓒ   short

4   The game _____ good.

  Ⓕ   was

  Ⓖ   were

  Ⓗ   be

5   Barb and Reggie _____ .

  Ⓐ   in the park

  Ⓑ   running fast

  Ⓒ   went home

6   This coat is the _____ one I ever had.

  Ⓕ   warm

  Ⓖ   warmest

  Ⓗ   warmer

STOP

Examples   **Directions:** Choose the sentence that is written correctly.

This one has been done for you.	Practice on this one.
C Ⓐ These cookies are good.	D Ⓕ A tallest tree is over there.
Ⓑ That are a funny story.	Ⓖ The grass is most greenest.
Ⓒ My friends is here.	Ⓗ That is the prettiest flower.

Do numbers 7-14 the same way.

7 Ⓐ Three dogs chases the ball.

Ⓑ My kitten likes to play.

Ⓒ I has no pets.

8 Ⓕ We walk to school.

Ⓖ The bus come late this morning.

Ⓗ My teacher drive to school.

9 Ⓐ Donna and Archie are young than I am.

Ⓑ Who is the faster runner in your class?

Ⓒ I am the oldest girl in my family.

10 Ⓕ Most of the people is in a good mood.

Ⓖ Many people are shopping today.

Ⓗ Many cars was in the parking lot.

11 Ⓐ Your shirt looks nice.

Ⓑ Your shoes gets muddy.

Ⓒ Ann find a hat.

12 Ⓕ This room is small than that one.

Ⓖ Your house is newest than mine.

Ⓗ The lights are bright in the kitchen.

13 Ⓐ Yesterday will be cold.

Ⓑ Tomorrow it will rain.

Ⓒ Today are too hot to play in the yard.

14 Ⓕ Bob stand under the tree.

Ⓖ Max and Irma sits on the log.

Ⓗ Will sat down.

STOP

Examples   **Directions:** Look at the underlined part of the sentence. Which pronoun could be substituted for the underlined word?

This one has been done for you.	Practice on this one.
A Did you see <u>Ruth</u>?	B Give <u>the birds</u> some food.
Ⓐ her	Ⓕ they
Ⓑ him	Ⓖ it
Ⓒ she	Ⓗ them

Do numbers 1-6 the same way.

   **The right answer means the same thing as the underlined part.**

1   <u>Earl and I</u> drew pictures of our friends.

Ⓐ They

Ⓑ Them

Ⓒ We

2   <u>Our car</u> is dirty.

Ⓕ We

Ⓖ It

Ⓗ They

3   Did you play with <u>my brother</u>?

Ⓐ them

Ⓑ her

Ⓒ him

4   That pretty horse belongs to <u>Jane and Harish</u>.

Ⓕ them

Ⓖ it

Ⓗ they

5   Will you let <u>Stan and me</u> go to the library?

Ⓐ us

Ⓑ him

Ⓒ her

6   <u>The plane</u> is loud.

Ⓕ He

Ⓖ She

Ⓗ It

STOP

Examples   **Directions:** Look at the sentences. Which one is a complete sentence? Choose the best answer.

The first one has been done for you.	Practice on this one.
A We were hungry.	**B** That book is good.
Ⓐ Hungry were we?	Ⓕ Is good that book?
⬤ Were we hungry?	Ⓖ Good is that book?
Ⓒ Were hungry we?	Ⓗ Is that book good?

 **Say each answer choice to yourself.**

Do numbers 1-6 the same way.

Practice

1   That clown is funny.

Ⓐ   Funny is that clown?

Ⓑ   Clown that is funny?

Ⓒ   Is that clown funny?

2   Her name is Mimi.

Ⓕ   Is name her Mimi?

Ⓖ   Is her name Mimi?

Ⓗ   Is Mimi name her?

3   They are going fishing.

Ⓐ   Are going they fishing?

Ⓑ   Going are they fishing?

Ⓒ   Are they going fishing?

4   An owl is in that tree.

Ⓕ   Is an owl in that tree?

Ⓖ   In that tree is an owl?

Ⓗ   Is in that tree an owl?

5   We will walk in the park.

Ⓐ   Will we walk in the park?

Ⓑ   Will walk we in the park?

Ⓒ   Walk in the park will we?

6   Fran was in the yard.

Ⓕ   In the yard was Fran?

Ⓖ   Was Fran in the yard?

Ⓗ   Was in the yard Fran?

STOP

Examples

Directions: Which of these is a full sentence? The first one has been done for you. Do numbers 7 and 8 the same way.

Directions: Look at the sentence. Is it correct as it is written? Choose the sentence, or if the sentence is correct, choose "the way it is." The first one has been done for you. Do numbers 9 and 10 the same way.

C Ⓐ To the beach.

    ❶ The wind is blowing.

    Ⓒ In the room on the floor.

D *The children play in the park.*

    Ⓕ Play in the park the children.

    Ⓖ The children in the park play.

    ❶ The way it is

---

7 Ⓐ Going to school.

    Ⓑ In the morning.

    Ⓒ The bus is late.

8 Ⓕ The dog is on the bed.

    Ⓖ Cats running up the steps.

    Ⓗ Fish and birds for pets.

9 Ⓐ Getting dressed.

    Ⓑ We are going to a party.

    Ⓒ A gift for my friend.

10 Ⓕ Lucy finished her homework.

    Ⓖ Kim and her brother.

    Ⓗ Studying at night.

Directions: Read or listen to the story. Choose the best answer to the question.

The Big Game

Our school had a football game.
The game on Friday.
It was very exciting.
We won the game.
Everyone was happy.

Which one is <u>not</u> a complete sentence?

Should the underlined sentence be changed or is it correct the way it is?

11 Ⓐ Our school had a football game.

    Ⓑ The game on Friday.

    Ⓒ It was very exciting.

12 Ⓕ We the game won.

    Ⓖ The game we won.

    Ⓗ The way it is

Example   **Directions:** Look at the sentences below. The sentences form a paragraph. A paragraph is a group of sentences about the same topic. Choose the sentence that best completes the paragraph. The first one has been done for you.

A   Our class went to the zoo yesterday.
We saw many animals.
_____ .

Ⓐ   I like going to school.

Ⓑ   It snowed last week.

Ⓒ   We heard the lions roar.

 **The correct answer fits best with the other sentences.**

Do numbers 1-4 the same way.

Practice

1   It rained all day.
My brother and I stayed home.
_____ .

Ⓐ   We live in the city.

Ⓑ   We played games and read.

Ⓒ   The store was crowded.

3   I like this book.
It is about space.
_____ .

Ⓐ   My sister gave me the book.

Ⓑ   My sister's name is Kim.

Ⓒ   The stars are far away.

2   A bird lives in our tree.
It built a nest.
_____ .

Ⓕ   Our yard is very large.

Ⓖ   Birds can fly.

Ⓗ   Soon there will be baby birds.

4   Jack has a dog.
The dog likes to play.
_____ .

Ⓕ   Jack lives near me.

Ⓖ   The dog chases a ball.

Ⓗ   Some people have cats.

STOP

Directions: Look at the sentences. There is a word missing in each one. Choose the word that best completes the sentence. The first one has been done for you. Do numbers 1-4 the same way.

Directions: Read the sentences. Which one in each group is a correct sentence? Choose the best answer. The first one has been done for you. Do numbers 5-8 the same way.

E1 Brenda _____ in the lake.

Ⓐ swim

Ⓑ swimming

● swims

E2 Ⓕ Four book are on the table.

● The light is bright.

Ⓗ A chair are there.

---

1 We live on a _____ street.

Ⓐ more busier

Ⓑ busy

Ⓒ busiest

2 _____ ran in the field.

Ⓕ Two horses

Ⓖ Quickly

Ⓗ Over there

3 Sue _____ her mother.

Ⓐ calling

Ⓑ call

Ⓒ called

4 Three big _____ were in the water.

Ⓕ boat

Ⓖ boats

Ⓗ bat

5 Ⓐ Ed jumps high.

Ⓑ We runs far.

Ⓒ Gail like to hike.

6 Ⓕ My drawing is the funny.

Ⓖ Her story is most longest.

Ⓗ This is the newest toy.

7 Ⓐ Yesterday they will walk to the park.

Ⓑ Tomorrow we will drive to the lake.

Ⓒ We are hope to go for a hike in the woods.

8 Ⓕ The kitten played with the paper cup.

Ⓖ A kittens is sleeping on the chair.

Ⓗ My cat had five kitten last week.

STOP

Directions: Look at the sentence. Choose the word from the list that means the same thing as the underlined words. Practice on the first one. Then do numbers 9-11 the same way.

Directions: Look at the sentence. Think about how that sentence could be turned into a question. Choose the best answer. Practice on the first one. Then do numbers 12-14 the same way.

E3 The lot was full of cars.

 Ⓐ He

 Ⓑ It

 Ⓒ She

E4 Her rabbit is black.

 Ⓕ Is black her rabbit?

 Ⓖ Is her black rabbit?

 Ⓗ Is her rabbit black?

---

9 Did you see my mother at the park?

 Ⓐ them

 Ⓑ she

 Ⓒ her

12 Grace will come with us.

 Ⓕ Will Grace come with us?

 Ⓖ With us will come Grace?

 Ⓗ Will with us come Grace?

10 Val and I are going to ride our bikes.

 Ⓕ We

 Ⓖ It

 Ⓗ They

13 The fire is warm.

 Ⓐ Is warm the fire?

 Ⓑ Is fire the warm?

 Ⓒ Is the fire warm?

11 Will you help Mike wash the dishes?

 Ⓐ he

 Ⓑ him

 Ⓒ her

14 Our car is broken.

 Ⓕ Is broken our car?

 Ⓖ Is our car broken?

 Ⓗ Is car our broken?

STOP

Directions: Read each sentence. Choose the one that is a complete sentence. Practice on the first one. Then do numbers 15 and 16 the same way.

Directions: Look at the sentences below. The sentences form a paragraph. A paragraph is a group of sentences that all have to do with the same thing. Which sentence could be added to complete the paragraph? Practice on the first one. Then do number 17 the same way.

E5 (A) I dropped my pen.
    (B) A pencil on the desk.
    (C) In the room on the floor.

E6 Matt is very happy.
    He got a new puppy.
    _____ .

    (F) Matt has friends.
    (G) Puppies like bones.
    (H) The puppy likes to play.

15 (A) Visiting his friend.
    (B) A newspaper on the ground.
    (C) Bert walked down the street.

16 (F) We drank milk.
    (G) Eating cookies.
    (H) Cutting the apple.

17 Amy helped her father.
    First she washed the dishes.
    _____ .

    (A) Her father is a police officer.
    (B) Then she cleaned her room.
    (C) Then she got out of bed.

Directions: Read or listen to this story.

The Funny Rabbit

A rabbit live in our yard.
       (1)
He is a funny rabbit.
Seeing our dog.
The rabbit tries to play with him.
We all laugh at the rabbit.

Look at the underlined word. What should that word be?

18 (F) living
    (G) lives
    (H) It is correct.

Which one is not a complete sentence?

19 (A) Seeing our dog.
    (B) The rabbit tries to play with him.
    (C) We all laugh at the rabbit.

STOP

NUMBER RIGHT _____

Lesson 13   Spelling Skills

Examples   **Directions:** Look at the words below. Which word is spelled correctly? Choose the best answer.

A This one has been done for you.	**B** Practice on this one.
mann man mahn	all al oll
Ⓐ **Ⓑ** Ⓒ	Ⓕ Ⓖ Ⓗ

 **If you are not sure which answer is correct, take your best guess.**

Do numbers 1-8 the same way.

Practice

1

    hant   hnd   hand

    Ⓐ   Ⓑ   Ⓒ

2

    fire   fir   fier

    Ⓕ   Ⓖ   Ⓗ

3

    nothin   nothing   noting

    Ⓐ   Ⓑ   Ⓒ

4

    sleep   slepe   sleap

    Ⓕ   Ⓖ   Ⓗ

5

    alang   along   ulong

    Ⓐ   Ⓑ   Ⓒ

6

    gam   gaim   game

    Ⓕ   Ⓖ   Ⓗ

7

    winther   wintr   winter

    Ⓐ   Ⓑ   Ⓒ

8

    story   storee   stawry

    Ⓕ   Ⓖ   Ⓗ

STOP

Examples   **Directions:** Look at the words. Which word is not spelled correctly?

C This one has been done for you.	**D** Practice on this one.
A Brng	**F** lost
B bag	**G** neu
C with	**H** hat

Do numbers 9-16 the same way.

9
- **A** This
- **B** samall
- **C** room

10
- **F** drov
- **G** clean
- **H** car

11
- **A** left
- **B** house
- **C** wun

12
- **F** any
- **G** mawr
- **H** paint

13
- **A** have
- **B** sand
- **C** shews

14
- **F** under
- **G** tall
- **H** trea

15
- **A** There
- **B** ise
- **C** lake

16
- **F** Whech
- **G** girl
- **H** first

STOP

Directions: Look at the words. Which one is spelled correctly?

E1 This one has been done for you.	E2 Practice on this one.
taday tooday today	word werd wird
Ⓐ Ⓑ **Ⓒ**	Ⓕ Ⓖ Ⓗ

Do numbers 1-10 the same way.

1

way   wae   wey

Ⓐ   Ⓑ   Ⓒ

6

cawrn   corn   korn

Ⓕ   Ⓖ   Ⓗ

2

sawng   sonk   song

Ⓕ   Ⓖ   Ⓗ

7

bloo   blu   blue

Ⓐ   Ⓑ   Ⓒ

3

lst   last   lasst

Ⓐ   Ⓑ   Ⓒ

8

must   mst   moust

Ⓕ   Ⓖ   Ⓗ

4

from   frum   ferum

Ⓕ   Ⓖ   Ⓗ

9

seet   sete   seat

Ⓐ   Ⓑ   Ⓒ

5

eech   each   eatch

Ⓐ   Ⓑ   Ⓒ

10

tal   tail   tayl

Ⓕ   Ⓖ   Ⓗ

STOP

Directions: Look at the words. Which word is <u>not</u> spelled correctly?

E3 This one has been done for you.	**E4** Practice on this one.
Ⓐ buy	Ⓕ walk
⬤ cote	Ⓖ hill
Ⓒ store	Ⓗ neer

Do numbers 11-18 the same way.

11

Ⓐ tired

Ⓑ sit

Ⓒ rst

12

Ⓕ sau

Ⓖ pig

Ⓗ farm

13

Ⓐ naim

Ⓑ pet

Ⓒ dog

14

Ⓕ Did

Ⓖ lok

Ⓗ door

15

Ⓐ Thank

Ⓑ nice

Ⓒ wach

16

Ⓕ wand

Ⓖ play

Ⓗ snow

17

Ⓐ are

Ⓑ goyng

Ⓒ home

18

Ⓕ When

Ⓖ read

Ⓗ papir

STOP

NUMBER RIGHT _____

Lesson 15   Study Skills

Example   **Directions:** Look at the words below. Which word comes first in ABC order? Choose the best answer.

king
Ⓐ

more
Ⓑ

grow
Ⓒ

 **Stay with your first answer choice.**

Practice

Read or listen to the sentence. Choose the best answer to each question.

1   Esteban is writing a story about his mother's job. What will help him with the report?

Ⓐ   remembering the names of his brothers and sisters

Ⓑ   asking his friends about the work their parents do

Ⓒ   remembering what his mother told him about her job

2   What will he put in the report that will tell others about his mother's job?

Ⓕ   tell what his mother likes to read

Ⓖ   tell about the kind of work his mother does

Ⓗ   tell what kind of sports his mother likes

Table of Contents
1. Where She Works 2
2. What She Does 4
3. When She Works 7
4. Who She Works With 10

Esteban has made a table of contents for his book. Look at the table of contents. Choose the best answer for these questions:

3   On which page did Esteban begin his story?

Ⓐ   2

Ⓑ   4

Ⓒ   7

4   Which chapter will tell about the hours and days that Esteban's mother works?

Ⓕ   1

Ⓖ   2

Ⓗ   3

Directions: Read or listen to the sentences. Choose the best answer to each question.

E1 Laura's class is writing about airplanes. She wants to write a story about a plane trip she took with her family. Which of these would help Laura most before she begins to write?

   Ⓐ thinking about what her teacher said about planes

   Ⓑ remembering what the plane trip was like

   Ⓒ asking friends if they have ever been on a plane

---

1 Laura is looking up these words in the dictionary. Which one will come first?

   Ⓐ airplane

   Ⓑ again

   Ⓒ also

2 Why is Laura writing her story? What is her purpose?

   Ⓕ tell about what she did on a plane trip

   Ⓖ tell about how a plane is built

   Ⓗ tell how high planes can fly

3 Which of these does not belong in Laura's story?

   Ⓐ what it was like getting on the plane

   Ⓑ how it felt to take off

   Ⓒ what kind of suitcase she has

Table of Contents

1. In The Airport 3
2. Taking Off 5
3. How It Feels to Fly 8
4. Landing 9

4 Look at Laura's table of contents. On which page did she begin her story?

   Ⓕ 3

   Ⓖ 5

   Ⓗ 8

5 Which chapter will tell about the end of Laura's plane trip?

   Ⓐ 2

   Ⓑ 3

   Ⓒ 4

STOP

To the Student:

These tests will give you a chance to put the tips you have learned to work.

A few last reminders . . .

- Be sure you understand all the directions before you begin each test. You may ask the teacher questions about the directions if you do not understand them.
- Work as quickly as you can during each test.
- When you change an answer, be sure to erase your first mark completely.

- You can guess at an answer or skip difficult items and go back to them later.
- Use the tips you have learned whenever you can.
- It is OK to be a little nervous. You may even do better.

Now that you have completed the lessons in this unit, you are on your way to scoring high!

STUDENT'S NAME		SCHOOL
LAST	FIRST	MI	TEACHER

FEMALE ○   MALE ○

BIRTH DATE

MONTH	DAY	YEAR
JAN ○	⓪ ⓪	⓪
FEB ○	① ①	①
MAR ○	② ②	②
APR ○	③ ③	③
MAY ○	④	④
JUN ○	⑤	⑤ ⑤
JUL ○	⑥	⑥ ⑥
AUG ○	⑦	⑦ ⑦
SEP ○	⑧	⑧ ⑧
OCT ○	⑨	⑨ ⑨
NOV ○		
DEC ○		

GRADE

Ⓚ ① ②

(Student name grid: columns of bubbles lettered A through Z)

PART 1   LISTENING

E1 Ⓐ Ⓑ Ⓒ	6 Ⓕ Ⓖ Ⓗ	12 Ⓕ Ⓖ Ⓗ	18 Ⓕ Ⓖ Ⓗ
1 Ⓐ Ⓑ Ⓒ	7 Ⓐ Ⓑ Ⓒ	13 Ⓐ Ⓑ Ⓒ	19 Ⓐ Ⓑ Ⓒ
2 Ⓕ Ⓖ Ⓗ	8 Ⓕ Ⓖ Ⓗ	14 Ⓕ Ⓖ Ⓗ	20 Ⓕ Ⓖ Ⓗ
3 Ⓐ Ⓑ Ⓒ	9 Ⓐ Ⓑ Ⓒ	15 Ⓐ Ⓑ Ⓒ	21 Ⓐ Ⓑ Ⓒ
4 Ⓕ Ⓖ Ⓗ	10 Ⓕ Ⓖ Ⓗ	16 Ⓕ Ⓖ Ⓗ	
5 Ⓐ Ⓑ Ⓒ	11 Ⓐ Ⓑ Ⓒ	17 Ⓐ Ⓑ Ⓒ	

PART 2   LANGUAGE MECHANICS

E1 Ⓐ Ⓑ Ⓒ	1 Ⓐ Ⓑ Ⓒ	12 Ⓕ Ⓖ Ⓗ	23 Ⓐ Ⓑ Ⓒ
E2 Ⓕ Ⓖ Ⓗ	2 Ⓕ Ⓖ Ⓗ	13 Ⓐ Ⓑ Ⓒ	24 Ⓕ Ⓖ Ⓗ
E3 Ⓐ Ⓑ Ⓒ	3 Ⓐ Ⓑ Ⓒ	14 Ⓕ Ⓖ Ⓗ	25 Ⓐ Ⓑ Ⓒ
E4 Ⓕ Ⓖ Ⓗ	4 Ⓕ Ⓖ Ⓗ	15 Ⓐ Ⓑ Ⓒ	
E5 Ⓐ Ⓑ Ⓒ	5 Ⓐ Ⓑ Ⓒ	16 Ⓕ Ⓖ Ⓗ	
E6 Ⓕ Ⓖ Ⓗ	6 Ⓕ Ⓖ Ⓗ	17 Ⓐ Ⓑ Ⓒ	
E7 Ⓐ Ⓑ Ⓒ	7 Ⓐ Ⓑ Ⓒ	18 Ⓕ Ⓖ Ⓗ	
E8 Ⓕ Ⓖ Ⓗ	8 Ⓕ Ⓖ Ⓗ	19 Ⓐ Ⓑ Ⓒ	
E9 Ⓐ Ⓑ Ⓒ	9 Ⓐ Ⓑ Ⓒ	20 Ⓕ Ⓖ Ⓗ	
E10 Ⓕ Ⓖ Ⓗ	10 Ⓕ Ⓖ Ⓗ	21 Ⓐ Ⓑ Ⓒ	
E11 Ⓐ Ⓑ Ⓒ	11 Ⓐ Ⓑ Ⓒ	22 Ⓕ Ⓖ Ⓗ	

PART 3   LANGUAGE EXPRESSION

E1 Ⓐ Ⓑ Ⓒ	2 Ⓕ Ⓖ Ⓗ	7 Ⓐ Ⓑ Ⓒ	12 Ⓕ Ⓖ Ⓗ
E2 Ⓕ Ⓖ Ⓗ	3 Ⓐ Ⓑ Ⓒ	8 Ⓕ Ⓖ Ⓗ	13 Ⓐ Ⓑ Ⓒ
E3 Ⓐ Ⓑ Ⓒ	4 Ⓕ Ⓖ Ⓗ	9 Ⓐ Ⓑ Ⓒ	
E4 Ⓕ Ⓖ Ⓗ	5 Ⓐ Ⓑ Ⓒ	10 Ⓕ Ⓖ Ⓗ	
1 Ⓐ Ⓑ Ⓒ	6 Ⓕ Ⓖ Ⓗ	11 Ⓐ Ⓑ Ⓒ	

PART 4   SPELLING

E1 Ⓐ Ⓑ Ⓒ	3 Ⓐ Ⓑ Ⓒ	9 Ⓐ Ⓑ Ⓒ	15 Ⓐ Ⓑ Ⓒ
E2 Ⓕ Ⓖ Ⓗ	4 Ⓕ Ⓖ Ⓗ	10 Ⓕ Ⓖ Ⓗ	16 Ⓕ Ⓖ Ⓗ
E3 Ⓐ Ⓑ Ⓒ	5 Ⓐ Ⓑ Ⓒ	11 Ⓐ Ⓑ Ⓒ	17 Ⓐ Ⓑ Ⓒ
E4 Ⓕ Ⓖ Ⓗ	6 Ⓕ Ⓖ Ⓗ	12 Ⓕ Ⓖ Ⓗ	18 Ⓕ Ⓖ Ⓗ
1 Ⓐ Ⓑ Ⓒ	7 Ⓐ Ⓑ Ⓒ	13 Ⓐ Ⓑ Ⓒ	
2 Ⓕ Ⓖ Ⓗ	8 Ⓕ Ⓖ Ⓗ	14 Ⓕ Ⓖ Ⓗ	

PART 5   STUDY SKILLS

E1 Ⓐ Ⓑ Ⓒ
1 Ⓐ Ⓑ Ⓒ
2 Ⓕ Ⓖ Ⓗ
3 Ⓐ Ⓑ Ⓒ
4 Ⓕ Ⓖ Ⓗ
5 Ⓐ Ⓑ Ⓒ

STOP

Part 1 Listening

Directions: Read or listen to each story. Choose the best answer for each question. The first one has been done for you. Do numbers 1-8 the same way.

E1 Pedro's class was studying history. They went to an old fort, an old barn, and a house. Which was the first place that Pedro visited?

Ⓐ

Ⓑ

Ⓒ

---

1 Some friends were talking about different sports. Alberta likes an exciting sport she does in the water. Ned likes a sport he can play with other people on a big field. Adrian likes a sport she can do on wheels. What sport does Alberta like?

Ⓐ

Ⓑ

Ⓒ

---

2 Evan is thinking about a piece of clothing. You put your feet into it one at a time and it covers your legs. Which piece of clothing is Evan thinking of?

Ⓕ

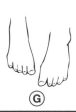
Ⓖ

Ⓗ

---

3 Margo was studying feathers. She learned that feathers are used by birds to make their nests and by people to make pillows. Which thing is used to make the two other things?

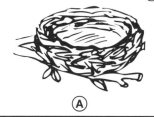
Ⓐ

Ⓑ

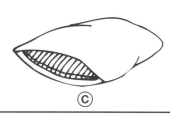
Ⓒ

---

4 Vince helped his mother build a shelf. His mother put something on the shelf. Which thing would Vince's mother put on the shelf?

Ⓕ

Ⓖ

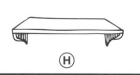
Ⓗ

GO ▷

5 A group of people went to a nature center on a winter day. They saw a fox and a bear. They also saw something that children had built. It made them laugh. What thing made them laugh?

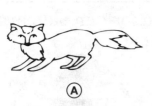

Ⓐ

Ⓑ

Ⓒ

---

6 Jerry and his grandfather went to the museum. At the museum, Jerry's grandfather showed him something he had used years ago. What did Jerry's grandfather show him?

Ⓕ

Ⓖ

Ⓗ

---

7 Cindy was walking home from school. She heard a buzzing sound and saw something fly by. What did she see?

Ⓐ

Ⓑ

Ⓒ

---

8 Ted was looking for something on his father's desk. He was having a hard time because the thing he was looking for was smaller than everything else on the desk. What was Ted looking for?

Ⓕ

Ⓖ

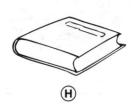

Ⓗ

STOP

Directions: Read or listen to the story. Choose the best answer.

E2 On his way home from school, Ross stopped at the library. He found Mr. Smith, who helped Ross on the computer. Then he helped him use the encyclopedia on the computer. What did Ross use at the library?

(F) a book

(G) a video

(H) a computer

E3 Squirrels do funny things. They gather nuts in the fall and bury them in the ground. Then they dig them up and eat them. Sometimes, they forget where the nuts were buried. These nuts grow into trees. That's why squirrels are sometimes called nature's farmers. What are squirrels compared to in the story?

(A) builders

(B) farmers

(C) cooks

9 Last May, Jennie's class visited Washington, D.C. They saw many government buildings and museums. They even visited the White House. When did Jennie's class visit Washington?

(A) May

(B) October

(C) March

10 Cindy was going to her first baseball game with her parents. They were going to see the Chicago Cubs. She couldn't wait! What kind of game was Cindy seeing?

(F) football game

(G) basketball game

(H) baseball game

11 How did Cindy feel about going to the game?

(A) excited

(B) tired

(C) angry

12 Jeff had been saving his money for a new bike for a long time. Whenever he received money for a birthday or holiday, he put it in the bank. He was saving for a new bike. What was Jeff saving for?

(F) glove

(G) basketball

(H) bike

13 One day, Penny saw a strange bird. She told her teacher, who said it was a thrasher. The bird got its name because it looks for food in piles of dead leaves. What kind of bird did Penny see?

(A) robin

(B) thrasher

(C) cardinal

14 Where do thrashers look for food?

(F) piles of leaves

(G) small puddles

(H) large trees

STOP

Directions: Look at each part of the sentence. Does either part of the sentence need a capital letter? Choose the part of the sentence that needs a capital letter. If neither part needs a capital letter, choose None.

This one has been done for you.

E1   Tell sharon | we will be late.   None
    Ⓐ   Ⓑ   Ⓒ

Practice on this one.

E2   Our house | was painted white.   None
    Ⓕ   Ⓖ   Ⓗ

Do numbers 1-6 the same way.

1   We live | in utah.   None
   Ⓐ   Ⓑ   Ⓒ

2   Mina and i | went skating.   None
    Ⓕ   Ⓖ   Ⓗ

3   These shoes | are new.   None
    Ⓐ   Ⓑ   Ⓒ

4   is this | your pen?   None
   Ⓕ   Ⓖ   Ⓗ

5   My dog | likes cookies.   None
   Ⓐ   Ⓑ   Ⓒ

6   The bank is closed | next monday.   None
      Ⓕ   Ⓖ   Ⓗ

STOP

Directions: For E3, read or listen to the story. Choose the best answer to the question. Do numbers 7 and 8 the same way. For E4 and E5, mark the circle for the word in the sentence that should begin with a capital letter. Do numbers 9-12 the same way.

E3	Pablo is writing a story about what he did over the weekend. How should Pablo have written the underlined part?	**E4**	We went to the library on thursday.

E3 Pablo is writing a story about what he did over the weekend. How should Pablo have written the underlined part?

We went for a walk.
It was a nice day.
_____
(1)

Ⓐ nice Day
Ⓑ Nice day
Ⓒ The way he did

E4 We went to the library on thursday.

Ⓕ went
Ⓖ library
Ⓗ thursday

E5 did you bring your sled?

Ⓐ did
Ⓑ bring
Ⓒ sled?

Read this letter.

A Letter to Cindy

Dear Cindy,

how are you?
_____
(1)
I like my new teacher.

His name is Mr. Walker.
_____
(2)

Look at the first underlined part. How should it be written?

7 Ⓐ How are
   Ⓑ How Are
   Ⓒ The way it is

Look at the second underlined part. How should it be written?

8 Ⓕ mr. walker
   Ⓖ Mr. walker
   Ⓗ The way it is

9 Our family went camping in june.
   Ⓐ family
   Ⓑ camping
   Ⓒ june

10 i can see the stars.
   Ⓕ i
   Ⓖ can
   Ⓗ stars

11 that note is for the teacher.
   Ⓐ that
   Ⓑ note
   Ⓒ teacher

12 Did you give ray his money?
   Ⓕ give
   Ⓖ ray
   Ⓗ money

STOP

99

Directions: Look at the sentence. Fill in the circle beside the punctuation mark that is needed in the sentence. If no more punctuation marks are needed, mark None. The first one has been done for you. Practice on the next two. Then do numbers 13-19 the same way.

E6   Where are your socks?

  Ⓕ .   Ⓖ !   ❶ None

E7   Where is the ice

  Ⓐ   ice.

  Ⓑ   ice?

  Ⓒ   ice!

E8   We had fun at the zoo

  Ⓕ   zoo.

  Ⓖ   zoo?

  Ⓗ   zoo!

13   This is good bread

  Ⓐ .   Ⓑ ?   Ⓒ None

14   Who will help Joyce

  Ⓕ !   Ⓖ ?   Ⓗ None

15   There is a lot of traffic today.

  Ⓐ ?   Ⓑ !   Ⓒ None

16   Will Raffi go with us

  Ⓕ   us.

  Ⓖ   us!

  Ⓗ   us?

17   I forgot my lunch money today

  Ⓐ   today!

  Ⓑ   today.

  Ⓒ   today?

18   Bring the present to the party

  Ⓕ   party!

  Ⓖ   party?

  Ⓗ   party.

19   Hurry or we'll miss the bus

  Ⓐ   bus!

  Ⓑ   bus.

  Ⓒ   bus?

STOP

Directions: Look at the underlined sentence. What punctuation goes at the end? This one has been done for you. Do numbers 20 & 21 the same way.

Directions: Look at the sentences. Do they need capital letters or punctuation? Choose the sentence that needs a capital letter or punctuation. Do numbers 22-25 the same way.

E9 *This is a heavy log*
        (1)
  I hope we can move it.

Ⓐ log?
Ⓑ log!
Ⓒ log.

E10 Ⓕ i called my mother.
     Ⓖ She said I could go.
     Ⓗ Will you come with me

E11 Ⓐ Bing ran fast.
     Ⓑ he was late.
     Ⓒ His friends laughed?

I have many new friends. I like my school a lot
                              (1)

Don't worry. You are still my best friend.
 (2)

I hope to see you soon.

20 What punctuation goes at the end of the first underlined sentence?
Ⓕ lot.
Ⓖ lot!
Ⓗ lot?

21 How should the second underlined word be written?
Ⓐ Do'nt
Ⓑ Dont
Ⓒ The way it is

22 Ⓕ Can I come in.
        Ⓖ Walk this way
        Ⓗ This room is pretty.

24 Ⓕ our school is far away.
        Ⓖ The bus is full.
        Ⓗ Can i sit here?

23 Ⓐ Who is that?
        Ⓑ This is my friend
        Ⓒ Her name is jamie.

25 Ⓐ Where were you on monday.
        Ⓑ Wednesday is my birthday.
        Ⓒ They will leave Tomorrow

STOP

Directions: Look at the sentence. Choose the word or words that best completes the sentence. The first one has been done for you. Do numbers 1 and 2 the same way.

E1   My sister _____ .
- Ⓐ   being there
- Ⓑ   very quickly
- **Ⓒ**   won a contest

Directions: Look at the sentences. Which one is written correctly? The first one has been done for you. Do numbers 3 and 4 the same way.

E2   Ⓕ   The clock are slow.
- **Ⓖ**   We waited two days.
- Ⓗ   They drove for five hour.

---

1   The frogs _____ into the pond.
- Ⓐ   jumps
- Ⓑ   jumped
- Ⓒ   jumping

2   Her _____ always get cold.
- Ⓕ   ears
- Ⓖ   ear
- Ⓗ   err

3   Ⓐ   She made more better soup.
- Ⓑ   This pie tastes gooder.
- Ⓒ   That is the biggest apple.

4   Ⓕ   They will buy a new house next month.
- Ⓖ   Next week they left.
- Ⓗ   Last year I will go to the fair with my friends.

Look at the underlined part of the sentence. What pronoun could be substituted for the words? Do numbers 5 and 6 the same way.

5   We gave Art and Cathy our old sofa.
- Ⓐ   them
- Ⓑ   it
- Ⓒ   they

6   My bike got dirty.
- Ⓕ   We
- Ⓖ   They
- Ⓗ   It

Look at the sentence. Could you turn the sentence into a question? Choose the best question. Do numbers 7 and 8 the same way.

7   Jed will return tomorrow.
- Ⓐ   Will tomorrow return Jed?
- Ⓑ   Will Jed return tomorrow?
- Ⓒ   Will Jed tomorrow return?

8   That camera is mine.
- Ⓕ   Is mine that camera?
- Ⓖ   Mine is that camera?
- Ⓗ   Is that camera mine?

STOP

Directions: Which one is a full sentence? Choose the best answer. This one has been done for you. Do numbers 9 and 10 the same way.

E3   Ⓐ   Learning about oceans.

    ❸   Larry wrote a story.

    Ⓒ   To read it to the class.

Directions: Which sentence should come next in this paragraph? Choose the best answer. Practice on this one. Do number 11 the same way.

E4   Pat was happy.
    He caught a fish.
    _____ .

    Ⓕ   His sister is younger.

    Ⓖ   He went fishing.

    Ⓗ   It was very big.

9   Ⓐ   Starting to purr.

    Ⓑ   To give it food.

    Ⓒ   They found a lost cat.

10   Ⓕ   The leaves fell from the tree.

    Ⓖ   My favorite season.

    Ⓗ   Getting colder after summer.

11   This is Ida's book.
    She forgot it.
    _____ .

    Ⓐ   Ida was here.

    Ⓑ   She will come back for it.

    Ⓒ   The book is here.

Read or listen to the story.

New Friends

Daisy <u>walked</u> to the park.
    (1)

She met a girl named Paula.
They played with a ball.
The park is near the school.
Daisy and Paula became good friends.

How should the underlined part of the sentence be written?

12   Ⓕ   walking

    Ⓖ   walk

    Ⓗ   the way it is

If you were writing a story, which sentence would you leave out?

13   Ⓐ   She met a girl named Paula.

    Ⓑ   The park is near the school.

    Ⓒ   Daisy and Paula became good friends.

STOP

Directions: Look at the words. Which word is spelled correctly? Mark your choice.

E1	This one has been done for you.			E2	Practice on this one.		
	dirk	darc	dark		away	awa	awai
	Ⓐ	Ⓑ	●		Ⓕ	Ⓖ	Ⓗ

Do numbers 1–10 the same way.

1

clock	clok	klock
Ⓐ	Ⓑ	Ⓒ

2

gled	clad	glad
Ⓕ	Ⓖ	Ⓗ

3

lonk	long	lawng
Ⓐ	Ⓑ	Ⓒ

4

heid	hide	hyde
Ⓕ	Ⓖ	Ⓗ

5

booth	bowth	both
Ⓐ	Ⓑ	Ⓒ

6

muv	move	moov
Ⓕ	Ⓖ	Ⓗ

7

rock	rok	rack
Ⓐ	Ⓑ	Ⓒ

8

sadd	sed	sad
Ⓕ	Ⓖ	Ⓗ

9

stret	street	strete
Ⓐ	Ⓑ	Ⓒ

10

part	parrt	pahrt
Ⓕ	Ⓖ	Ⓗ

STOP

Directions: Look at the words. Which word is <u>not</u> spelled correctly? Mark your choice.

E3 This one has been done for you.	E4 Practice on this one.
Ⓐ how	Ⓕ kolor
● ryde	Ⓖ old
Ⓒ horse	Ⓗ bike

Do numbers 11-18 the same way.

11

Ⓐ made
Ⓑ bed
Ⓒ befor

12

Ⓕ Evry
Ⓖ class
Ⓗ happy

13

Ⓐ hit
Ⓑ bal
Ⓒ bat

14

Ⓕ cowl
Ⓖ ate
Ⓗ field

15

Ⓐ water
Ⓑ lake
Ⓒ werm

16

Ⓕ taruck
Ⓖ stop
Ⓗ road

17

Ⓐ find
Ⓑ bigg
Ⓒ shell

18

Ⓕ mutch
Ⓖ toy
Ⓗ cost

STOP

Directions: Read or listen to the story. Find the best answer for each question.

E1   Horace and his friends went on a trip to the nature center. The next day, his teacher asked the children to write a story about something new they learned at the nature center.

Horace is looking up these words in the dictionary. Which word comes first in A-B-C order?

leaf	lake	lunch
Ⓐ	Ⓑ	Ⓒ

---

1   How should Horace get ideas for his story?

   Ⓐ   draw a picture of the nature center

   Ⓑ   think about what he wore to the nature center

   Ⓒ   make a list of things he saw at the nature center

2   What will help Horace write his story?

   Ⓕ   reading the children's guide he received at the nature center

   Ⓖ   visiting a store that sells bird seed and feeders

   Ⓗ   asking his mother what she likes about the nature center

3   Which sentence does not belong in Horace's story?

   Ⓐ   I learned about different kinds of trees.

   Ⓑ   My sister's name is Terry.

   Ⓒ   Some birds do not go south in the winter.

Here is Horace's table of contents.

Table of Contents

1. Birds............................2
2. Trees............................3
3. Fish............................5
4. Animals........................9

4   Horace saw a beaver and a fox at the nature center. In which chapter should he write about them?

   Ⓕ   2

   Ⓖ   3

   Ⓗ   4

5   On which page will Horace begin his story?

   Ⓐ   2

   Ⓑ   3

   Ⓒ   5

STOP

Table of Contents
Math

Lesson 1   Numeration

Example   **Directions:** Look at the picture. Then answer the question. The first one has been done for you.

A   Which tree is the shortest tree?

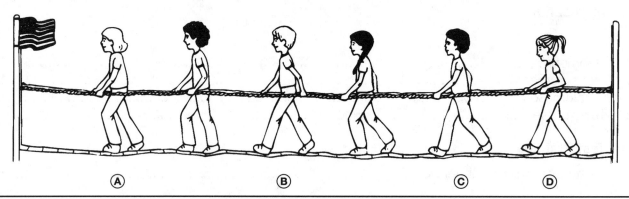

Ⓐ   Ⓑ   Ⓒ

**Tips**   **Look at all the answer choices before you mark the one you think is correct.**

Practice

1   Which hiker is the sixth hiker from the flag?

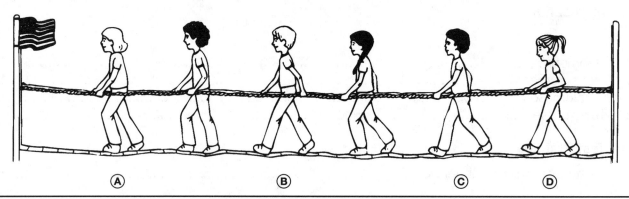

Ⓐ   Ⓑ   Ⓒ   Ⓓ

2   How many ears of corn are there in all?

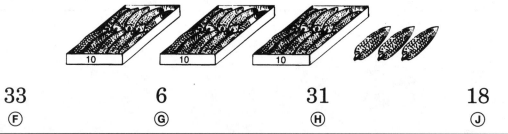

33   6   31   18
Ⓕ   Ⓖ   Ⓗ   Ⓙ

3   Which pot has the fewest flowers?

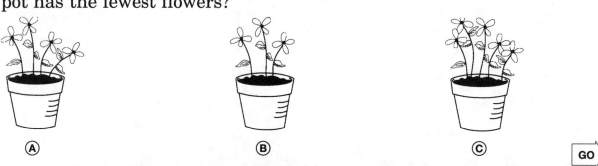

Ⓐ   Ⓑ   Ⓒ

GO

4   Which number means 7 tens and 3 ones?

10	7103	73	731
Ⓕ	Ⓖ	Ⓗ	Ⓙ

---

5   Which picture shows the ball above the seal?

Ⓐ   Ⓑ   Ⓒ

---

6   Which one shows the expanded numeral for two-hundred and forty-six?

200 + 40 + 6	2000 + 46	246 + 100	2 + 100 + 46
Ⓕ	Ⓖ	Ⓗ	Ⓙ

---

7   Look at the bowling pins. Find the one in the box. Which place is it from the start?

    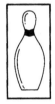

first	fourth	fifth	third
Ⓐ	Ⓑ	Ⓒ	Ⓓ

---

8   How many sticks are there in all?

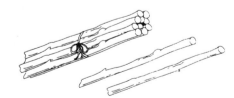

ten	seven	three	twelve
Ⓕ	Ⓖ	Ⓗ	Ⓙ

STOP

Example   **Directions:** Look at the pictures. Choose the best answer to the
question. The first one has been done for you.

A   How many fish are there in the bowl?

3
Ⓐ

6
🅑

5
Ⓒ

   **If you are not sure of an answer, take your best guess.**

Do numbers 1-9 the same way.

Practice

---

1   Which picture shows the feathers in order from smallest to largest?

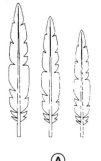
Ⓐ

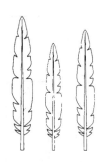
Ⓑ

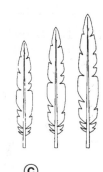
Ⓒ

---

2   If you are counting by ones, which number comes after 26?

27
Ⓕ

26
Ⓖ

25
Ⓗ

36
Ⓙ

---

3   Which pattern needs the number 4 in the blank space?

0, 1, 2, ___
Ⓐ

2, 3, ___ , 5
Ⓑ

___ , 6, 7, 8
Ⓒ

5, ___ , 7, 8
Ⓓ

---

4   Which group of nails has three more than the number in the box?

3

Ⓕ

Ⓖ

Ⓗ

GO ▷

5 Which number is missing in this pattern?

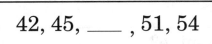

42, 45, ____ , 51, 54

46	50	48	49
Ⓐ	Ⓑ	Ⓒ	Ⓓ

6 Which group of canes has two more than the number of hats?

Ⓕ	Ⓖ	Ⓗ	Ⓙ

7 How many pillows are there on top of the bed?

6	5	11	7
Ⓐ	Ⓑ	Ⓒ	Ⓓ

8 Which number is more than 4 but less than 8?

3	7	10	9
Ⓕ	Ⓖ	Ⓗ	Ⓙ

9 Look at the numbers in the box. Think how they would be arranged from least to greatest. Which number below would come fourth?

217, 270, 207, 273, 237

273	237	207	270
Ⓐ	Ⓑ	Ⓒ	Ⓓ

STOP

Example   **Directions:** Look at the question. Then choose the best answer. The first one has been done for you.

A   Which number is twenty-nine?

209   29   20   39

Ⓐ   🅑   ©   Ⓓ

 **Mark your answer choice carefully. Be sure the space you fill in is for the answer you think is correct.**

Do numbers 1-10 the same way.
Practice

1   How many pears are there?

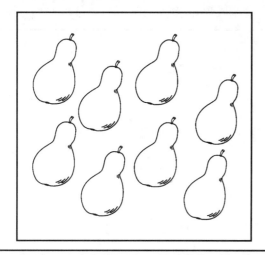

5   10   8

Ⓐ   Ⓑ   ©

2   How many dots are there in the top box?

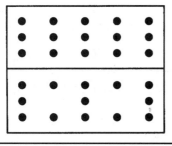

13   15   12

Ⓕ   Ⓖ   Ⓗ

3   Look at the number in the box. Which picture matches the number?

11

Ⓐ   Ⓑ   ©   GO

4 Which number is eighty-three?

83	8	38	89
Ⓕ	Ⓖ	Ⓗ	Ⓙ

5 There were five birds. Two flew away. How many were left?

$$5 + 2 = \qquad 5 - 2 = \qquad 2 - 5 =$$

Ⓐ Ⓑ Ⓒ

6 Which symbol makes this sentence true?

$$248 \bigcirc 5$$

=	>	<
Ⓕ	Ⓖ	Ⓗ

7 Which number matches the word in the box?

seventy	70	7	17
	Ⓐ	Ⓑ	Ⓒ

8 Which number sentence does not belong with the others?

$3 + 9 = 12$	$9 + 3 = 12$	$12 - 9 = 3$	$9 - 3 = 6$
Ⓕ	Ⓖ	Ⓗ	Ⓙ

9 Look at the number sentence in the box. Which number will make the sentence true?

$$\square + 5 = 5$$

10	1	0	5
Ⓐ	Ⓑ	Ⓒ	Ⓓ

10 Which number statement is the same as thirteen plus eight?

$8 + 13$	$1 + 38$	$18 - 3$	$8 - 13$
Ⓕ	Ⓖ	Ⓗ	Ⓙ

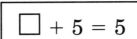

Example   **Directions:** Look at the picture. Choose the best answer to the question. The first one has been done for you.

A   Which square is divided exactly in half?

Ⓐ   Ⓑ   Ⓒ   Ⓓ

Sometimes it helps to say numbers to yourself before choosing an answer.

Do numbers 1-8 the same way.

Practice

1   Look at the pattern in the box. Which group has that same pattern?

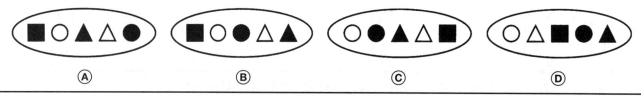

Ⓐ   Ⓑ   Ⓒ   Ⓓ

2   Look at the pattern in the box. Which object will come next in the pattern?

Ⓕ   Ⓖ   Ⓗ   Ⓙ

3   Look at the pattern in the box. If you count by fives, what number should come next?

| 35 | ___ | 45 | 50 |

40   30   54   55
Ⓐ   Ⓑ   Ⓒ   Ⓓ   GO

4   Which number has one ten and nine ones?

    91   19   110   9

    Ⓕ   Ⓖ   Ⓗ   Ⓙ

5   Which box has one-third of the balloons shaded?

      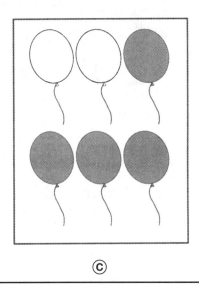

       Ⓐ   Ⓑ   Ⓒ

6   Look at the pattern in the box. Which shape will complete the pattern?

        Ⓕ   Ⓖ   Ⓗ   Ⓙ

7   How many tens and ones are there in ninety-five?

   9 tens and   5 tens and   90 tens and   95 tens and
     5 ones   9 ones   5 ones   5 ones

      Ⓐ   Ⓑ   Ⓒ   Ⓓ

8   What number comes after forty when you count by tens?

    10   140   50   40

    Ⓕ   Ⓖ   Ⓗ   Ⓙ

Directions: Look at the picture. Then choose the best answer to the question. The first one has been done for you.

E1 Which building has the most windows?

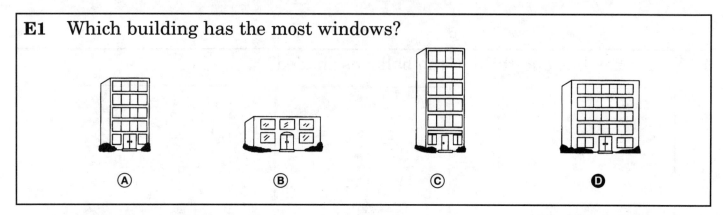

Ⓐ   Ⓑ   Ⓒ   **Ⓓ**

Do numbers 1-10 in the same way.

---

1 Which chalkboard is divided exactly in half?

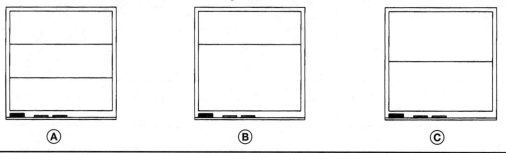

Ⓐ   Ⓑ   Ⓒ

---

2 Which number is less than twenty-seven?

121	28	24	31
Ⓕ	Ⓖ	Ⓗ	Ⓙ

---

3 Which number is forty-three?

43	34	403	48
Ⓐ	Ⓑ	Ⓒ	Ⓓ

---

4 Look at the pattern in the box. Which shape should come next in the pattern?

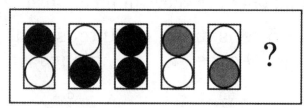

Ⓕ   Ⓖ   Ⓗ   Ⓙ

GO

5 When you count by fives, you go, "Five, ten, fifteen, twenty, twenty-five . . . ."
Which number would come next?

30	20	5	525
Ⓐ	Ⓑ	Ⓒ	Ⓓ

6 Which fish is third from the plant?

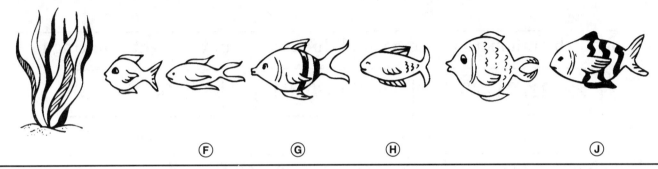

	Ⓕ	Ⓖ	Ⓗ	Ⓙ

7 There are two ants on a hill and four beside it. Which number sentence tells
how many ants there are in all?

2 + 2 =	4 − 2 =	2 − 4 =	2 + 4 =
Ⓐ	Ⓑ	Ⓒ	Ⓓ

8 How many tens and ones are there in seventy-two?

2 tens and 7 ones	70 tens and 2 ones	7 tens and 2 ones	20 tens and 7 ones
Ⓕ	Ⓖ	Ⓗ	Ⓙ

9 Look at the number in the box. Which word has exactly this many letters
in it?

9	beautiful	happy	joyful
	Ⓐ	Ⓑ	Ⓒ

10 Which answer shows the expanded numeral for one hundred thirty-one?

100 + 30 + 1	13 + 1	1 + 31	100 + 3 + 1
Ⓕ	Ⓖ	Ⓗ	Ⓙ

GO

11 Look at the ones and tens chart. What number does it show?

TENS	ONES
///	//

30   32   23   5

Ⓐ   Ⓑ   Ⓒ   Ⓓ

12 Look at the numbers in the boxes. Which one is in the right counting order?

22, 21, 24, 23   77, 79, 80, 81   62, 63, 64, 65

Ⓕ   Ⓖ   Ⓗ

13 Which group has exactly two shoes for each child?

Ⓐ   Ⓑ   Ⓒ   Ⓓ

14 Which circle is divided into four equal parts?

Ⓕ   Ⓖ   Ⓗ   Ⓙ

15 Eight people are waiting for a bus. Three of them get on the first bus. Which number sentence shows how many people waited for the second bus?

8 − 3 =   8 + 3 =   8 − 1 =   3 − 8 =

Ⓐ   Ⓑ   Ⓒ   Ⓓ

16 Look at the circles and the box. Which number shows how many circles are <u>inside</u> the box?

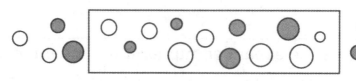

5   12   7   13

Ⓕ   Ⓖ   Ⓗ   Ⓙ

GO

17 Look at the number pattern in the box. Which word shows the number that is missing from the pattern?

8, 9, 10, ___ , 12, 13

ten	fourteen	eleven	twelve
Ⓐ	Ⓑ	Ⓒ	Ⓓ

18 Look at each box. Which box does <u>not</u> have a total of six brushes?

      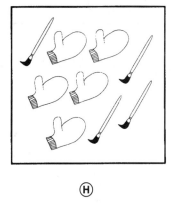

Ⓕ   Ⓖ   Ⓗ

19 Look at the crown in the box. Look at the sun. Which place is the crown in the box from the sun?

fourth	fifth	second	first
Ⓐ	Ⓑ	Ⓒ	Ⓓ

20 Which number is between 38 and 44?

31	40	45	29
Ⓕ	Ⓖ	Ⓗ	Ⓙ

21 Look at the number statement in the box. What sign will make the statement true?

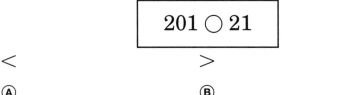

201 ◯ 21

<	>	=
Ⓐ	Ⓑ	Ⓒ

STOP

Lesson 6   Addition

Examples   **Directions:** Solve each addition problem. Choose the best answer.

A This one has been done for you.	**B** Practice on this one.
$\begin{array}{r} 3 \\ +2 \\ \hline \end{array}$ 1 Ⓐ 6 Ⓑ 5 **Ⓒ** 2 Ⓓ	$4 + 4 =$ 0 Ⓕ 4 Ⓖ 44 Ⓗ 8 Ⓙ

 **If a problem is too difficult, skip it and come back to it later if you have time.**

Do numbers 1-14 the same way.

Practice

1

$\begin{array}{r} 6 \\ +3 \\ \hline \end{array}$

1 Ⓐ
8 Ⓑ
3 Ⓒ
9 Ⓓ

4

$0 + 8 =$

0 Ⓕ
8 Ⓖ
18 Ⓗ
80 Ⓙ

2

$12 + 5 =$

17 Ⓕ
7 Ⓖ
18 Ⓗ
62 Ⓙ

5

$\begin{array}{r} 2 \\ 6 \\ +5 \\ \hline \end{array}$

8 Ⓐ
13 Ⓑ
11 Ⓒ
7 Ⓓ

3

$4 + 7 = \square$

3 Ⓐ
10 Ⓑ
11 Ⓒ
9 Ⓓ

6

$\begin{array}{r} 15 \\ +13 \\ \hline \end{array}$

28 Ⓕ
2 Ⓖ
18 Ⓗ
12 Ⓙ

GO

7

$7 + 7 = \square$

77 Ⓐ
0 Ⓑ
14 Ⓒ
16 Ⓓ

8

$8 + 1 + 3 = \square$

11 Ⓕ
19 Ⓖ
9 Ⓗ
12 Ⓙ

9

$$\begin{array}{r} 219 \\ +\ 41 \\ \hline \end{array}$$

178 Ⓐ
250 Ⓑ
260 Ⓒ
249 Ⓓ

10

$6 + 6 + 7 = \square$

5 Ⓕ
19 Ⓖ
12 Ⓗ
13 Ⓙ

11

$\square + 4 = 9$

3 Ⓐ
49 Ⓑ
13 Ⓒ
5 Ⓓ

12

$$\begin{array}{r} 120 \\ +\ 10 \\ \hline \end{array}$$

130 Ⓕ
110 Ⓖ
220 Ⓗ
121 Ⓙ

13

$$\begin{array}{r} 50 \\ +\ 9 \\ \hline \end{array}$$

51 Ⓐ
59 Ⓑ
41 Ⓒ
69 Ⓓ

14

$$\begin{array}{r} 17 \\ +16 \\ \hline \end{array}$$

33 Ⓕ
23 Ⓖ
1 Ⓗ
32 Ⓙ

STOP

Examples   **Directions:** Solve each subtraction problem. Choose the best answer.

This one has been done for you.	Practice on this one.
A	**B**
$4 - 1 =$	$10 - \square = 1$
14 (A)	9 (F)
2 (B)	11 (G)
5 (C)	6 (H)
3 **(D)**	19 (J)

 **Tips** You can eliminate answer choices that are larger than the numbers being subtracted. These answers cannot be correct.

Do numbers 1-14 the same way.

Practice

1

$9 - 8 =$

1 (A)
17 (B)
2 (C)
11 (D)

4

$\begin{array}{r} 6 \\ -\ 3 \\ \hline \end{array}$

63 (F)
9 (G)
3 (H)
36 (J)

2

$\begin{array}{r} 15 \\ -\ \ 6 \\ \hline \end{array}$

19 (F)
8 (G)
21 (H)
9 (J)

5

$17 - 12 = \square$

4 (A)
29 (B)
15 (C)
5 (D)

3

$\begin{array}{r} 54 \\ -\ 32 \\ \hline \end{array}$

23 (A)
22 (B)
32 (C)
12 (D)

6

$\begin{array}{r} 26 \\ -\ 17 \\ \hline \end{array}$

43 (F)
9 (G)
13 (H)
19 (J)

GO

7

$$81 - 9$$

90 Ⓐ
82 Ⓑ
72 Ⓒ
11 Ⓓ

11

$$78 - 7 = \square$$

8 Ⓐ
77 Ⓑ
71 Ⓒ
85 Ⓓ

8

$$11 - 8 = \square$$

3 Ⓕ
19 Ⓖ
2 Ⓗ
5 Ⓙ

12

$$558 - 52$$

56 Ⓕ
6 Ⓖ
506 Ⓗ
620 Ⓙ

9

$$63 - 11$$

74 Ⓐ
52 Ⓑ
25 Ⓒ
42 Ⓓ

13

$$8¢ - 2¢$$

28¢ Ⓐ
9¢ Ⓑ
10¢ Ⓒ
6¢ Ⓓ

10

$$48 - 24$$

60 Ⓕ
24 Ⓖ
72 Ⓗ
14 Ⓙ

14

$$7 - 7$$

0 Ⓕ
14 Ⓖ
1 Ⓗ
2 Ⓙ

STOP

Directions: Solve these addition and subtraction problems. Choose the best answer. If none of the answers is correct, choose "N."

This one has been done for you.	Practice on this one.
E1	**E2**

E1

$$2 + 2 =$$

2	22	0	N
Ⓐ	Ⓑ	Ⓒ	**Ⓓ**

E2

$$\begin{array}{r} 14 \\ -\ 13 \\ \hline \end{array}$$

1 Ⓕ
27 Ⓖ
17 Ⓗ
2 Ⓙ

Do numbers 1-18 the same way.

1 $7 + 3 = \square$

10	11	4	N
Ⓐ	Ⓑ	Ⓒ	Ⓓ

2 $4 + 5 = \square$

1	8	9	N
Ⓕ	Ⓖ	Ⓗ	Ⓙ

3 $6 + 7 = \square$

17	13	12	N
Ⓐ	Ⓑ	Ⓒ	Ⓓ

4 $9 - 1 = \square$

6	7	1	N
Ⓕ	Ⓖ	Ⓗ	Ⓙ

5 $5 - 2 = \square$

3	7	2	N
Ⓐ	Ⓑ	Ⓒ	Ⓓ

6 $12 - 10 = \square$

22	4	2	N
Ⓕ	Ⓖ	Ⓗ	Ⓙ

7

$$\begin{array}{r} 52 \\ +\ \ 2 \\ \hline \end{array}$$

54 Ⓐ
55 Ⓑ
48 Ⓒ
50 Ⓓ

8

$$36 - 10 = \square$$

36 Ⓕ
26 Ⓖ
16 Ⓗ
35 Ⓙ

9

$$\begin{array}{r} 2 \\ 7 \\ +\ 6 \\ \hline \end{array}$$

9 Ⓐ
51 Ⓑ
15 Ⓒ
19 Ⓓ

10

$$12 - 6 = \square$$

4 Ⓕ
5 Ⓖ
18 Ⓗ
6 Ⓙ

GO

11

$$25 + 1 = \square$$

24 Ⓐ
35 Ⓑ
26 Ⓒ
251 Ⓓ

15

$$\begin{array}{r} 29 \\ + 21 \\ \hline \end{array}$$

8 Ⓐ
50 Ⓑ
48 Ⓒ
13 Ⓓ

12

$$\begin{array}{r} 66 \\ - 55 \\ \hline \end{array}$$

11 Ⓕ
121 Ⓖ
56 Ⓗ
45 Ⓙ

16

$$\begin{array}{r} 38 \\ - 27 \\ \hline \end{array}$$

46 Ⓕ
55 Ⓖ
65 Ⓗ
11 Ⓙ

13

$$\begin{array}{r} 78\cent \\ - 23\cent \\ \hline \end{array}$$

11¢ Ⓐ
55¢ Ⓑ
45¢ Ⓒ
54¢ Ⓓ

17

$$\begin{array}{r} 45 \\ + 15 \\ \hline \end{array}$$

40 Ⓐ
70 Ⓑ
60 Ⓒ
10 Ⓓ

14

$$\begin{array}{r} 5 \\ 5 \\ + 5 \\ \hline \end{array}$$

10 Ⓕ
55 Ⓖ
25 Ⓗ
15 Ⓙ

18

$$17 - 8 = \square$$

9 Ⓕ
25 Ⓖ
3 Ⓗ
11 Ⓙ

STOP

NUMBER RIGHT _____

Lesson 9   Geometry

Example   **Directions:** Look at the picture. Choose the best answer to the question. The first one has been done for you.

A Which one shows a circle inside a square?

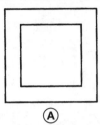 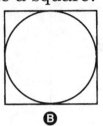 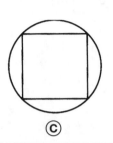

     Ⓐ   Ⓑ   Ⓒ

 **Tips**   Use key words, pictures, and numbers to help you find the right answer.

Do numbers 1-18 the same way.

Practice

---

1   Look at the shape in the box. Which picture is most like that shape?

  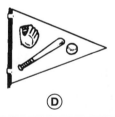

   Ⓐ   Ⓑ   Ⓒ   Ⓓ

---

2   Look at the shapes. Which one is different from the others?

   Ⓕ   Ⓖ   Ⓗ   Ⓙ

---

3   Look at the shapes. They can be folded on the dotted line. When you fold one shape, the two sides will match perfectly. Which picture shows the shape that has sides that will match when it is folded on the dotted line?

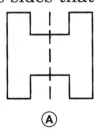 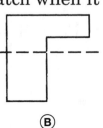 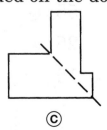 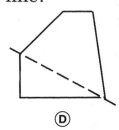

   Ⓐ   Ⓑ   Ⓒ   Ⓓ   GO▷

4   How many sides does a triangle have?

2   3   4   5
Ⓕ   Ⓖ   Ⓗ   Ⓙ

5   Which shape is exactly the same size and shape as the one at the beginning of the row?

      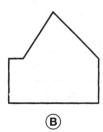   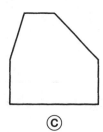   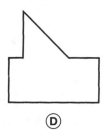

Ⓐ   Ⓑ   Ⓒ   Ⓓ

6   Look at the picture of the present in the box. Which shape looks the most like the present?

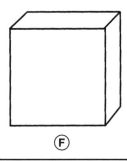   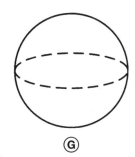   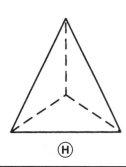   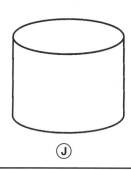

Ⓕ   Ⓖ   Ⓗ   Ⓙ

7   Look at the shapes in the box. How many rectangles are there?

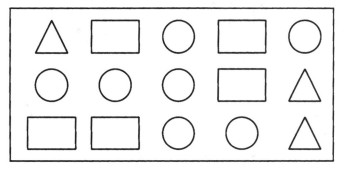

3   5   4   7
Ⓐ   Ⓑ   Ⓒ   Ⓓ

GO

8   Look at the shaded shape. How many sides does it have?

8	6	4	9
Ⓕ	Ⓖ	Ⓗ	Ⓙ

9   Look at the figure in the box. It shows half of a shape. Which picture shows the other half?

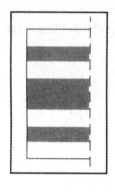         

Ⓐ   Ⓑ   Ⓒ

10   Look at the groups of lines. Which group could be joined to form a triangle?

      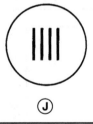   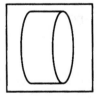

Ⓕ   Ⓖ   Ⓗ   Ⓙ

11   Look at the shape in the box. Which of the objects is <u>least</u> like that shape?

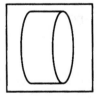         

Ⓐ   Ⓑ   Ⓒ

12   Which of these shapes is different from the others?

Ⓕ   Ⓖ   Ⓗ   Ⓙ

GO

13 Which group of shapes has the most triangles?

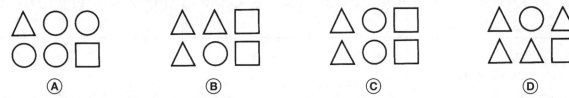

14 There are four groups of shapes. Which group has two different shapes?

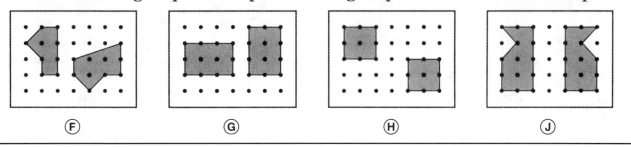

15 Which shape has the fewest sides?

16 Look at this puzzle: The button is <u>not</u> inside the square and it is <u>not</u> inside the circle. Which picture shows the answer to this puzzle?

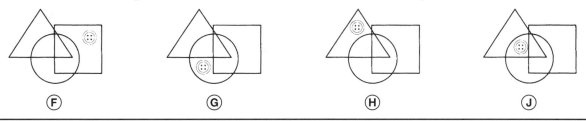

17 Look at the shape in the box. Which shape matches that shape?

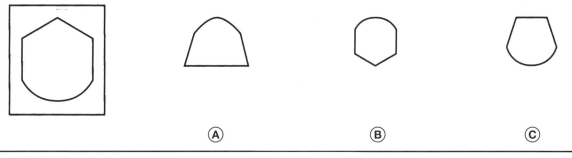

18 Look at the shapes inside the box. How many shapes have three sides?

5	4	2	3
Ⓕ	Ⓖ	Ⓗ	Ⓙ

STOP

Example   **Directions:** Look at the picture. Choose the best answer to the question.

This one has been done for you.

A Which coin is worth ten cents?

    Ⓐ   **Ⓑ**   Ⓒ   Ⓓ

 **Tips** **Listen carefully to the question while you look at the figure and answer choices for the problem.**

Do numbers 1-15 the same way.

Practice

1 Which object would you use to find out how much something weighs?

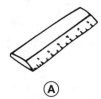   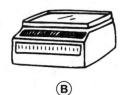      

   Ⓐ   Ⓑ   Ⓒ   Ⓓ

2 Look at the dog and the bones. Which number tells about how many bones long the dog is?

   5   3   9   7

   Ⓕ   Ⓖ   Ⓗ   Ⓙ

3 Look at the large block. About how many smaller blocks would equal the size of the larger block?

            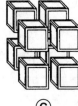

                  Ⓐ   Ⓑ   Ⓒ

GO

4 Look at the round clock. Which one shows the same time as the time on the round clock?

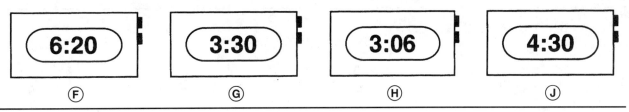

| 6:20 | 3:30 | 3:06 | 4:30 |
| F | G | H | J |

Look at the calendar. Answer questions 5-7.

OCTOBER						
SUN	MON	TUE	WED	THU	FRI	SAT
			1	2	3	4
5	6	7	8	9	10	11
12	13	14	15	16	17	18
19	20	21	22	23	24	25
26	27	28	29	30	31	

5 Which date is the first Tuesday in October?

October 1   October 9   October 14   October 7
  Ⓐ   Ⓑ   Ⓒ   Ⓓ

6 What day of the week is October 19?

Monday   Thursday   Sunday   Wednesday
  Ⓕ   Ⓖ   Ⓗ   Ⓙ

7 On what day of the week does November begin?

Saturday   Wednesday   Monday   Friday
  Ⓐ   Ⓑ   Ⓒ   Ⓓ

GO

8 Look at the pencil. How many centimeters long is the pencil?

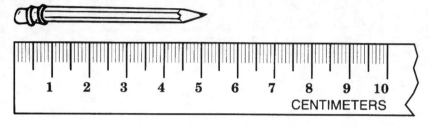

5	6	3	10
Ⓕ	Ⓖ	Ⓗ	Ⓙ

9 Which one is a nickel?

Ⓐ   Ⓑ   Ⓒ   Ⓓ

10 Ned went fishing at two o'clock. Two hours later he caught a fish. What time was it when he caught the fish?

Ⓕ   Ⓖ   Ⓗ   Ⓙ

11 Shannon wants to check the temperature of the pond. What should she use?

Ⓐ   Ⓑ   Ⓒ   Ⓓ

12 Wally went to a yard sale. He had a quarter. Which item could he buy?

30¢   50¢   20¢   40¢

Ⓕ   Ⓖ   Ⓗ   Ⓙ

GO

13   Look at the ruler and the pens. About how many inches long is the shortest pen?

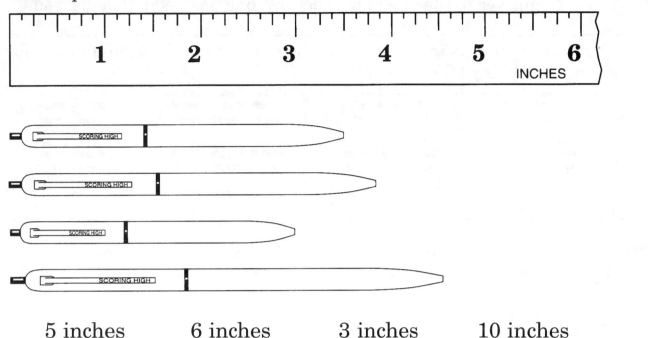

5 inches   6 inches   3 inches   10 inches
Ⓐ   Ⓑ   Ⓒ   Ⓓ

14   Cheryl's train leaves at 11. She wants to be there fifteen minutes early. What time will that be?

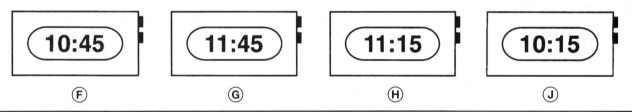

10:45   11:45   11:15   10:15
Ⓕ   Ⓖ   Ⓗ   Ⓙ

15   Look at each group of coins. Which one has a dime and a nickel in it?

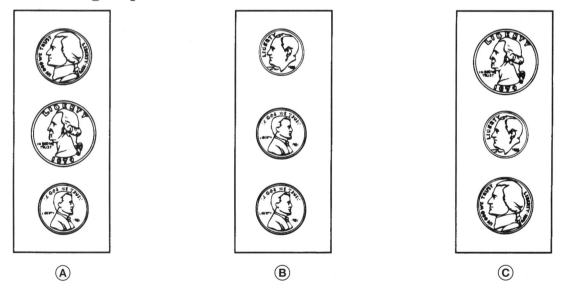

Ⓐ   Ⓑ   Ⓒ

Example   **Directions:** Read or listen to the story. Then choose the best answer to the question. The first one has been done for you.

A There were six tops in the store. Ted bought one for himself and one for his sister. How many tops were left?

Ⓐ   Ⓑ   Ⓒ   Ⓓ

 **Listen carefully to the question. Think about what you are supposed to do before you choose an answer.**

Do numbers 1-15 the same way.

Practice

1   A rancher had four white horses, eight gray horses, and three black horses. How many horses did he have in all?

12   15   11   9
Ⓐ   Ⓑ   Ⓒ   Ⓓ

2   Read or listen to the words in the box. Then choose the best answer to the question.

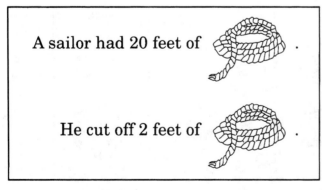

How many feet of rope were left?

2   22   18   17
Ⓕ   Ⓖ   Ⓗ   Ⓙ   GO

OBJECTS IN THE ATTIC

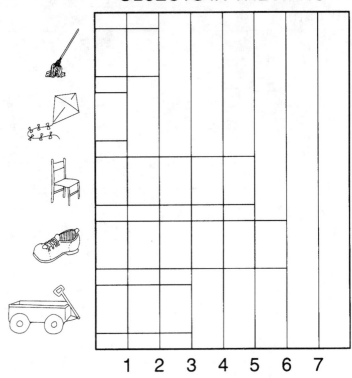

1 2 3 4 5 6 7

Look at the graph. The graph shows how many objects were stored in Kirstie's attic.

---

3 Find the object that there were three of in the attic.

Ⓐ

Ⓑ

Ⓒ

Ⓓ

---

4 Which group shows how many mops there were in the attic?

Ⓕ

Ⓖ

Ⓗ

Ⓙ

---

5 Which answer shows the total number of shoes and chairs in the attic?

5	11	6	12
Ⓐ	Ⓑ	Ⓒ	Ⓓ

GO ›

6 Look at the pots and pans in the box. Which picture shows how many more pots there are than pans?

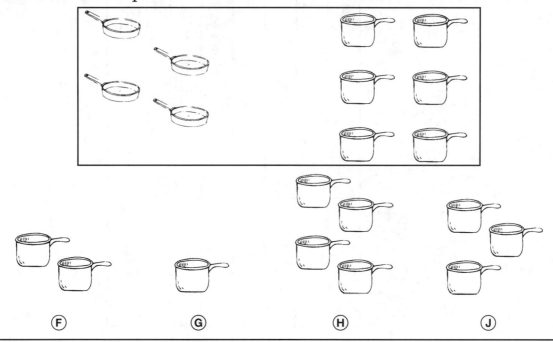

F   G   H   J

7 Darlene is eight years old. Her brother Kyle is two years older. How old is Kyle?

8   6   7   10

Ⓐ   Ⓑ   Ⓒ   Ⓓ

8 A parking lot has 12 cars in it. Five of the cars are driven away. How many cars are left? Which number sentence will help you find the answer?

Ⓕ $12 - 5 = \square$

Ⓖ $12 \times 5 = \square$

Ⓗ $12 + 5 = \square$

Ⓙ $12 \div 5 = \square$

9 A mall has 20 stores. Ten new stores were added to the mall. How many stores are there in all? Which number sentence will help you find the answer?

Ⓐ $20 \times 10 = \square$

Ⓑ $20 - 10 = \square$

Ⓒ $20 + 10 = \square$

Ⓓ $20 \div 10 = \square$

10 Eighteen people began a bicycle race. Only 15 finished. How many people did not finish the race? Which number sentence will help you find the answer?

Ⓕ $18 \div \square = 15$

Ⓖ $18 \times \square = 15$

Ⓗ $18 + \square = 15$

Ⓙ $18 - \square = 15$

11 A tree is 12 inches high in March. By August it has grown to 16 inches high. How much did it grow from March to August? Which number sentence will help you find the answer?

Ⓐ $12 - \square = 16$

Ⓑ $12 + \square = 16$

Ⓒ $\square + 16 = 12$

Ⓓ $12 + 16 = \square$

GO

TELEPHONE CALLS EACH DAY

MONDAY	☎ ☎ ☎
TUESDAY	☎ ☎
WEDNESDAY	☎ ☎
THURSDAY	☎ ☎ ☎ ☎
FRIDAY	☎ ☎ ☎ ☎ ☎

Look at this graph. It shows how many phone calls Rosa received in five days. Each picture of a telephone means one call.

---

12 Which group of telephones shows how many calls Rosa received on Thursday?

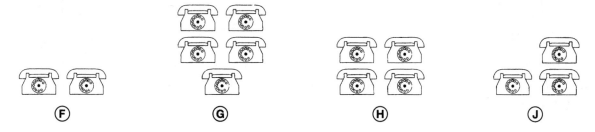

  Ⓕ   Ⓖ   Ⓗ   Ⓙ

---

13 On which day did Rosa receive the most calls?

Friday	Monday	Tuesday	Wednesday
Ⓐ	Ⓑ	Ⓒ	Ⓓ

---

14 How many calls did Rosa receive all together on Tuesday and Wednesday?

2	6	5	4
Ⓕ	Ⓖ	Ⓗ	Ⓙ

---

15 On Saturday, Rosa received eight calls. How many more calls did she receive on Saturday than on Friday?

8	3	5	4
Ⓐ	Ⓑ	Ⓒ	Ⓓ

STOP

Directions: Look at the picture. Choose the best answer to the question. The first one has been done for you.

E1

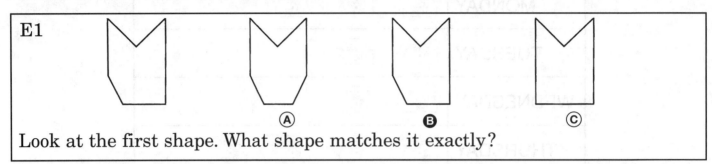

Look at the first shape. What shape matches it exactly?

---

1 Boris wants to buy a can of juice that costs 35 cents. Which group of coins is enough to buy the juice?

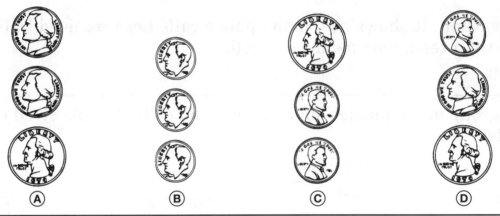

---

2 A flock of 20 geese are on a pond. Nine of them fly away. How many geese are left on the pond?

12	11	29	9
Ⓕ	Ⓖ	Ⓗ	Ⓙ

---

3 Look at the groups of shapes. Which group has exactly five circles and five squares?

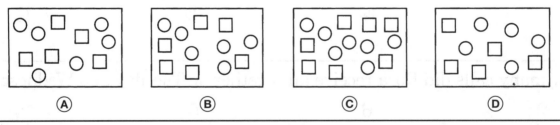

---

4 Gail's carpet is 6 feet long and 3 feet wide. Which one of these shapes is most like the carpet?

      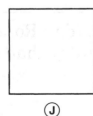

Ⓕ   Ⓖ   Ⓗ   Ⓙ

GO

5 Look at the round clock. Which clock shows the same time as the round clock?

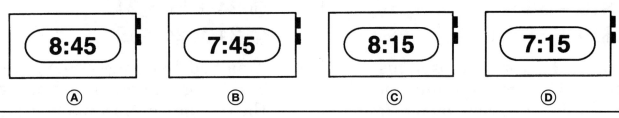

8:45	7:45	8:15	7:15
Ⓐ	Ⓑ	Ⓒ	Ⓓ

Look at the graph. The graph shows how many fish were caught by some friends.

NUMBER OF FISH CAUGHT

Dennis	🐟 🐟 🐟
Laurie	🐟 🐟 🐟 🐟 🐟
Megan	🐟 🐟
Martha	🐟 🐟
Carl	🐟

6 Who caught the most fish?

Martha	Carl	Dennis	Laurie
Ⓕ	Ⓖ	Ⓗ	Ⓙ

7 How many fish did Megan and Dennis catch altogether?

5	1	6	4
Ⓐ	Ⓑ	Ⓒ	Ⓓ

GO

8 Yvonne bought a book that cost eight dollars. She paid for it with a ten dollar bill. How much change did she get back? Which number sentence will help you find the answer?

(F) $\$10 \div \$8 = \square$

(G) $\$10 \times \$8 = \square$

(H) $\$10 - \$8 = \square$

(J) $\$10 + \$8 = \square$

9 Clark had seven stamps in his collection. He received nine more for his birthday. How many stamps did he have in all? Which number sentence will help you find the answer?

(A) $9 \times 7 = \square$

(B) $7 - 9 = \square$

(C) $9 \div 7 = \square$

(D) $7 + 9 = \square$

10 The distance from Lincoln's home to the beach is 24 miles. How far must Lincoln and his family travel to go to the beach and return home? Which number sentence will help you find the answer?

(F) $24 - 24 = \square$

(G) $24 \times \square = 24$

(H) $24 + \square = 24$

(J) $24 + 24 = \square$

11 Tina had 18 oranges. She gave 6 to her grandfather and brought the rest home. How many oranges did she bring home? Which number sentence will help you find the answer?

(A) $18 - 6 = \square$

(B) $18 \times \square = 6$

(C) $\square + 18 = 6$

(D) $18 + 6 = \square$

Look at the calendar.

JUNE						
SUN	MON	TUE	WED	THU	FRI	SAT
1	2	3	4	5	6	7
8	9	10	11	12	13	14
15	16	17	18	19	20	21
22	23	24	25	26	27	28
29	30					

12 Which day of the week is the last day of June?

Monday (F) Thursday (G) Tuesday (H) Wednesday (J)

13 On what day of the week does June twentieth fall?

Sunday (A) Thursday (B) Monday (C) Friday (D)

14 If you were going to start a vacation on the fourth Sunday in June, what day would you start your vacation?

June 29 (F) June 15 (G) June 22 (H) June 28 (J)

GO

15   Look at the ruler and the toy train. About how long is the toy train?

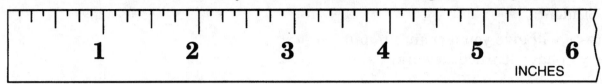

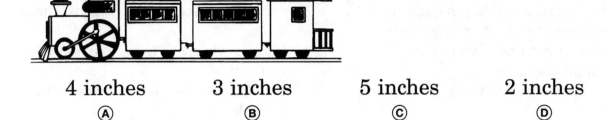

4 inches
Ⓐ

3 inches
Ⓑ

5 inches
Ⓒ

2 inches
Ⓓ

Look at the graph. The graph shows how many girls and boys in the class like different sports.

FAVORITE SPORTS

	FOOTBALL	TENNIS	SOCCER
GIRLS	2	7	5
BOYS	7	3	3

16   How many boys are there in the class?

7
Ⓕ

6
Ⓖ

4
Ⓗ

3
Ⓙ

17   How many girls and boys all together liked tennis?

8
Ⓐ

7
Ⓑ

9
Ⓒ

10
Ⓓ

18   How many girls are in the class?

14
Ⓕ

13
Ⓖ

9
Ⓗ

12
Ⓙ

STOP

NUMBER RIGHT _____

To the Student:

These tests will give you a chance to put the tips you have learned to work.

A few last reminders . . .

- Be sure you understand all the directions before you begin each test. You may ask the teacher questions about the directions if you do not understand them.
- Work as quickly as you can during each test.
- When you change an answer, be sure to erase your first mark completely.

- You can guess at an answer or skip difficult items and go back to them later.
- Use the tips you have learned whenever you can.
- It is OK to be a little nervous. You may even do better.

Now that you have completed the lessons in this unit, you are on your way to scoring high!

STUDENT'S NAME		SCHOOL
LAST	FIRST	MI	TEACHER

FEMALE ◯   MALE ◯

BIRTH DATE

MONTH	DAY		YEAR
JAN ◯	⓪ ⓪		⓪
FEB ◯	① ①		①
MAR ◯	② ②		②
APR ◯	③ ③		③
MAY ◯	④		④
JUN ◯	⑤	⑤	⑤
JUL ◯	⑥	⑥	⑥
AUG ◯	⑦	⑦	⑦
SEP ◯	⑧	⑧	⑧
OCT ◯	⑨	⑨	⑨
NOV ◯			
DEC ◯			

GRADE

Ⓚ   ①   ②

(Name grid with columns of bubbled letters A through Z)

PART 1 CONCEPTS

E1 Ⓐ Ⓑ Ⓒ Ⓓ	6 Ⓕ Ⓖ Ⓗ Ⓙ	12 Ⓕ Ⓖ Ⓗ Ⓙ	18 Ⓕ Ⓖ Ⓗ Ⓙ
1 Ⓐ Ⓑ Ⓒ Ⓓ	7 Ⓐ Ⓑ Ⓒ Ⓓ	13 Ⓐ Ⓑ Ⓒ Ⓓ	19 Ⓐ Ⓑ Ⓒ Ⓓ
2 Ⓕ Ⓖ Ⓗ Ⓙ	8 Ⓕ Ⓖ Ⓗ Ⓙ	14 Ⓕ Ⓖ Ⓗ Ⓙ	20 Ⓕ Ⓖ Ⓗ Ⓙ
3 Ⓐ Ⓑ Ⓒ Ⓓ	9 Ⓐ Ⓑ Ⓒ Ⓓ	15 Ⓐ Ⓑ Ⓒ Ⓓ	21 Ⓐ Ⓑ Ⓒ Ⓓ
4 Ⓕ Ⓖ Ⓗ Ⓙ	10 Ⓕ Ⓖ Ⓗ Ⓙ	16 Ⓕ Ⓖ Ⓗ Ⓙ	
5 Ⓐ Ⓑ Ⓒ Ⓓ	11 Ⓐ Ⓑ Ⓒ Ⓓ	17 Ⓐ Ⓑ Ⓒ Ⓓ	

PART 2 COMPUTATION

E1 Ⓐ Ⓑ Ⓒ Ⓓ	5 Ⓐ Ⓑ Ⓒ Ⓓ	11 Ⓐ Ⓑ Ⓒ Ⓓ	17 Ⓐ Ⓑ Ⓒ Ⓓ	23 Ⓐ Ⓑ Ⓒ Ⓓ
E2 Ⓕ Ⓖ Ⓗ Ⓙ	6 Ⓕ Ⓖ Ⓗ Ⓙ	12 Ⓕ Ⓖ Ⓗ Ⓙ	18 Ⓕ Ⓖ Ⓗ Ⓙ	24 Ⓕ Ⓖ Ⓗ Ⓙ
1 Ⓐ Ⓑ Ⓒ Ⓓ	7 Ⓐ Ⓑ Ⓒ Ⓓ	13 Ⓐ Ⓑ Ⓒ Ⓓ	19 Ⓐ Ⓑ Ⓒ Ⓓ	25 Ⓐ Ⓑ Ⓒ Ⓓ
2 Ⓕ Ⓖ Ⓗ Ⓙ	8 Ⓕ Ⓖ Ⓗ Ⓙ	14 Ⓕ Ⓖ Ⓗ Ⓙ	20 Ⓕ Ⓖ Ⓗ Ⓙ	26 Ⓕ Ⓖ Ⓗ Ⓙ
3 Ⓐ Ⓑ Ⓒ Ⓓ	9 Ⓐ Ⓑ Ⓒ Ⓓ	15 Ⓐ Ⓑ Ⓒ Ⓓ	21 Ⓐ Ⓑ Ⓒ Ⓓ	
4 Ⓕ Ⓖ Ⓗ Ⓙ	10 Ⓕ Ⓖ Ⓗ Ⓙ	16 Ⓕ Ⓖ Ⓗ Ⓙ	22 Ⓕ Ⓖ Ⓗ Ⓙ	

PART 3 APPLICATIONS

E1 Ⓐ Ⓑ Ⓒ Ⓓ	5 Ⓐ Ⓑ Ⓒ Ⓓ	10 Ⓕ Ⓖ Ⓗ Ⓙ	15 Ⓐ Ⓑ Ⓒ Ⓓ
1 Ⓐ Ⓑ Ⓒ Ⓓ	6 Ⓕ Ⓖ Ⓗ Ⓙ	11 Ⓐ Ⓑ Ⓒ Ⓓ	16 Ⓕ Ⓖ Ⓗ Ⓙ
2 Ⓕ Ⓖ Ⓗ Ⓙ	7 Ⓐ Ⓑ Ⓒ Ⓓ	12 Ⓕ Ⓖ Ⓗ Ⓙ	17 Ⓐ Ⓑ Ⓒ Ⓓ
3 Ⓐ Ⓑ Ⓒ Ⓓ	8 Ⓕ Ⓖ Ⓗ Ⓙ	13 Ⓐ Ⓑ Ⓒ Ⓓ	18 Ⓕ Ⓖ Ⓗ Ⓙ
4 Ⓕ Ⓖ Ⓗ Ⓙ	9 Ⓐ Ⓑ Ⓒ Ⓓ	14 Ⓕ Ⓖ Ⓗ Ⓙ	19 Ⓐ Ⓑ Ⓒ Ⓓ

Part 1   Concepts

Directions: Look at the picture. Choose the best answer to the question. This one has been done for you.

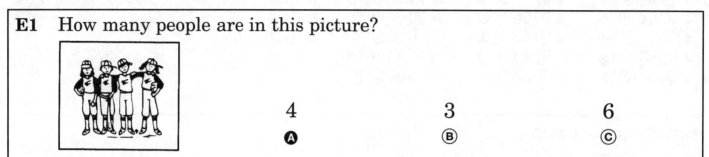

E1 How many people are in this picture?

    4   3   6
    Ⓐ   Ⓑ   Ⓒ

Do numbers 1-15 the same way.

1 Look at the number in the box. Which group of spoons matches that number?

12

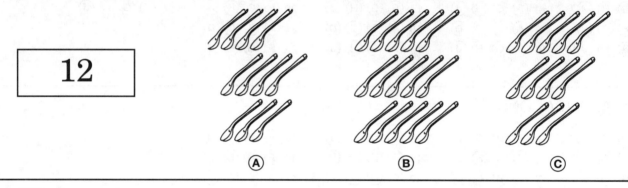

   Ⓐ   Ⓑ   Ⓒ

2 Which number comes just before 60?

  59   61   60   58
  Ⓕ   Ⓖ   Ⓗ   Ⓙ

3 Look at each group of hearts. In which group is the third heart from the bottom shaded?

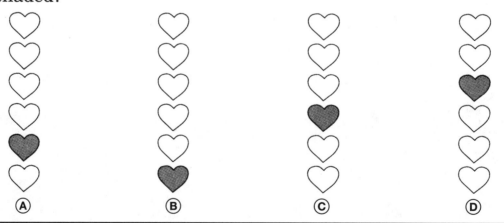

  Ⓐ   Ⓑ   Ⓒ   Ⓓ

4 Which shark is the shortest?

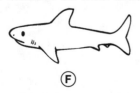 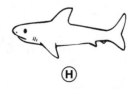

  Ⓕ   Ⓖ   Ⓗ

GO

5 Look at the numbers in the box. If you put them in counting order, which one would be fifth?

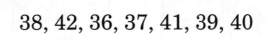

38, 42, 36, 37, 41, 39, 40

41	40	36	39
Ⓐ	Ⓑ	Ⓒ	Ⓓ

6 Which number is eighty-seven?

89	77	78	87
Ⓕ	Ⓖ	Ⓗ	Ⓙ

7 Which number should go where the circle is?

◇ **91 92** ◯ ☐ **95 96** △

97	94	93	90
Ⓐ	Ⓑ	Ⓒ	Ⓓ

8 Which picture shows the cat under the table?

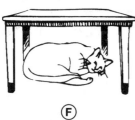  

Ⓕ   Ⓖ   Ⓗ

9 Which pattern needs the number twenty in the blank space?

___, 22, 23, 24   17, 18, 19, ___   21, ___, 23, 24
    Ⓐ   Ⓑ   Ⓒ

10 Which number sentence tells you how many more pins there are than bananas?

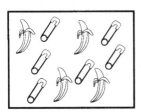

$6 - 4 =$ $6 + 4 =$ $10 - 0 =$
    Ⓕ   Ⓖ   Ⓗ

GO ▷

11 Which shape shows four equal parts?

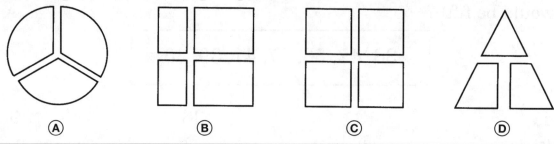

12 Look at the shapes in the box. Which shape occurs most frequently?

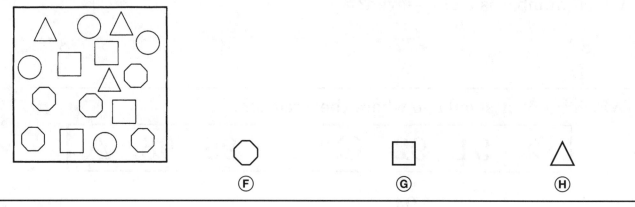

13 Look at the word in the box. How many letters does it have?

airplane	7	5	8
	Ⓐ	Ⓑ	Ⓒ

14 Look at the plates in the box. Which group of bowls has the same number as the plates?

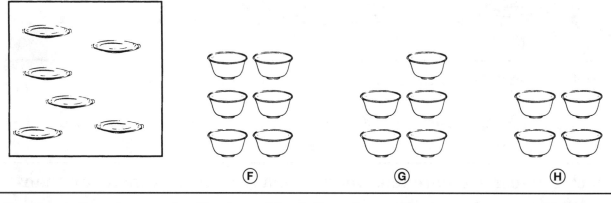

15 Look at the shapes in the box. Find the shape that comes next in the pattern.

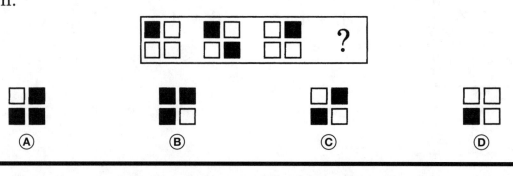

16 How many matches are there in all?

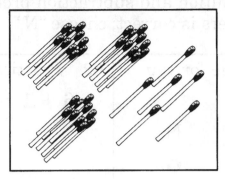

9	25	63	36
Ⓕ	Ⓖ	Ⓗ	Ⓙ

17 Which number is one less than fifty-four?

53	45	65	56
Ⓐ	Ⓑ	Ⓒ	Ⓓ

18 Which number is three hundred seventy-two?

327	372	273	272
Ⓕ	Ⓖ	Ⓗ	Ⓙ

19 Which number is ten more than the number in the box?

461	471	4610	561
	Ⓐ	Ⓑ	Ⓒ

20 Which symbol will make the number statement true?

$$77 \bigcirc 70 + 7$$

<	>	=
Ⓕ	Ⓖ	Ⓗ

21 What number matches the tens and ones chart?

TENS	ONES
///// /	////

514	46	64	55
Ⓐ	Ⓑ	Ⓒ	Ⓓ

STOP

Directions: Solve these addition and subtraction problems. Choose the best answer. If none of the answers is correct, choose "N."

E1 This one has been done for you.	**E2** Practice on this one.

E1   This one has been done for you.

$7 - 6 = \square$

13	4	0	N
Ⓐ	Ⓑ	Ⓒ	**Ⓓ**

E2   Practice on this one.

$6 + 1 = \square$

- 61 Ⓕ
- 5 Ⓖ
- 16 Ⓗ
- 7 Ⓙ

Do numbers 1-26 the same way.

1 $5 + 2 = \square$

8	3	7	N
Ⓐ	Ⓑ	Ⓒ	Ⓓ

2 $12 + 7 = \square$

19	5	16	N
Ⓕ	Ⓖ	Ⓗ	Ⓙ

3 $4 + 9 = \square$

5	12	11	N
Ⓐ	Ⓑ	Ⓒ	Ⓓ

4 $8 - 3 = \square$

6	5	11	N
Ⓕ	Ⓖ	Ⓗ	Ⓙ

5 $9 - 6 = \square$

14	15	2	N
Ⓐ	Ⓑ	Ⓒ	Ⓓ

6 $8 - 2 = \square$

4	6	10	N
Ⓕ	Ⓖ	Ⓗ	Ⓙ

7

$$\begin{array}{r} 31 \\ -\ 11 \\ \hline \end{array}$$

- 20 Ⓐ
- 10 Ⓑ
- 21 Ⓒ
- 42 Ⓓ

8

$6 + 17 = \square$

- 33 Ⓕ
- 23 Ⓖ
- 11 Ⓗ
- 57 Ⓙ

9

$$\begin{array}{r} 13 \\ +\ 22 \\ \hline \end{array}$$

- 53 Ⓐ
- 19 Ⓑ
- 9 Ⓒ
- 35 Ⓓ

10

$35 - 8 = \square$

- 17 Ⓕ
- 23 Ⓖ
- 27 Ⓗ
- 43 Ⓙ

GO

11

$$14¢ - 4¢ = \square$$

18¢ Ⓐ
10¢ Ⓑ
144¢ Ⓒ
54¢ Ⓓ

12

$$8¢ + 9¢ + 1¢ = \square$$

18¢ Ⓕ
19¢ Ⓖ
17¢ Ⓗ
20¢ Ⓙ

13

$$320$$
$$+ \ 52$$

327 Ⓐ
354 Ⓑ
273 Ⓒ
372 Ⓓ

14

$$70 - 40 = \square$$

110 Ⓕ
3 Ⓖ
30 Ⓗ
20 Ⓙ

15

$$\square + 6 = 11$$

5 Ⓐ
17 Ⓑ
4 Ⓒ
71 Ⓓ

16

$$209$$
$$- \ \ 9$$

119 Ⓕ
199 Ⓖ
200 Ⓗ
299 Ⓙ

17

$$100$$
$$+ \ 17$$

171 Ⓐ
117 Ⓑ
83 Ⓒ
207 Ⓓ

18

$$35¢$$
$$- 24¢$$

59¢ Ⓕ
1¢ Ⓖ
11¢ Ⓗ
21¢ Ⓙ

GO

19

$$700$$
$$- \underline{500}$$

200 Ⓐ
1200 Ⓑ
20 Ⓒ
750 Ⓓ

20

$$9 - 1 = \square$$

7 Ⓕ
19 Ⓖ
8 Ⓗ
10 Ⓙ

21

$$543$$
$$+ \underline{\ 21}$$

342 Ⓐ
664 Ⓑ
522 Ⓒ
564 Ⓓ

22

$$62 - \square = 58$$

5 Ⓕ
4 Ⓖ
120 Ⓗ
14 Ⓙ

23

$$\square - 10 = 27$$

7 Ⓐ
26 Ⓑ
17 Ⓒ
37 Ⓓ

24

$$15¢ + 7¢ = \square$$

85¢ Ⓕ
32¢ Ⓖ
22¢ Ⓗ
8¢ Ⓙ

25

$$2$$
$$10$$
$$+ \underline{\ 2}$$

12 Ⓐ
14 Ⓑ
16 Ⓒ
50 Ⓓ

26

$$14$$
$$+ \underline{11}$$

25 Ⓕ
3 Ⓖ
23 Ⓗ
52 Ⓙ

STOP

Example   **Directions:** Read or listen to each question. Mark the correct answer.

This one has been done for you.
E1   Tyler is watering plants. He has to water eight plants all together. He has watered five. How many more does he have to water?

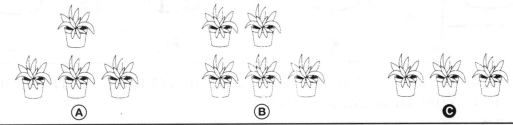

Ⓐ   Ⓑ   **Ⓒ**

Do numbers 1-15 the same way.

1   Lillian found 4¢. Sam found 5¢. How much did they find altogether? Which word sentence will help you find the answer?

Ⓐ   5¢ ÷ 4¢ = □
Ⓑ   4¢ × 5¢ = □
Ⓒ   5¢ − 4¢ = □
Ⓓ   4¢ + 5¢ = □

2   Nineteen people are in line for the movie. Fourteen are children. How many are adults? Which word sentence will help you find the answer?

Ⓕ   14 + 19 = □
Ⓖ   19 − 14 = □
Ⓗ   14 ÷ 19 = □
Ⓙ   19 × 14 = □

3   If a dog eats one pound of food in one day, how much will he eat in two days? Which word sentence will help you find the answer?

Ⓐ   1 − 1 = □
Ⓑ   1 × 1 = □
Ⓒ   1 + 2 = □
Ⓓ   1 + 1 = □

4   There are sixteen tomatoes in a bag. Twelve of them are ripe. How many are not ripe? Which word sentence will help you find the answer?

Ⓕ   16 ÷ 12 = □
Ⓖ   16 − □ = 12
Ⓗ   12 + 16 = □
Ⓙ   □ + 16 = 12

5   Look at each group of coins. Which group is worth the most?

Ⓐ   Ⓑ   Ⓒ

6   Four people got on an elevator. Then two more got on. Then five more got on. How many people in all were on the elevator?

11   10   7   9
Ⓕ   Ⓖ   Ⓗ   Ⓙ   GO

7 What cup is the same as the cup in the box?

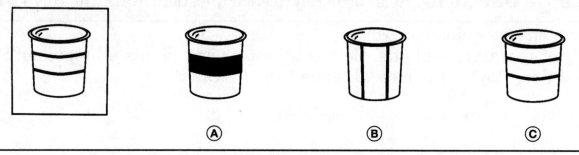

8 A train left the station at four o'clock. Five hours later, it arrived at its destination. What time did it arrive?

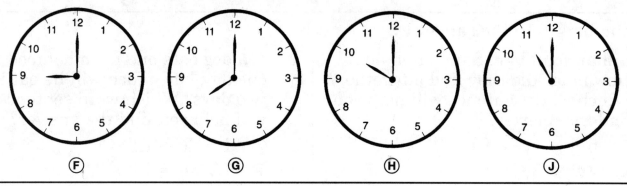

9 Look at these shapes. Which one can be folded in half so that the two parts match exactly?

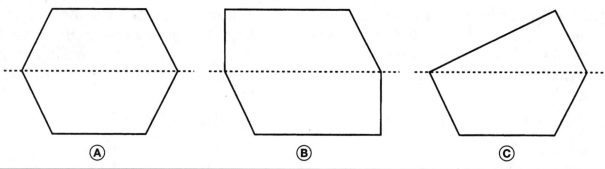

10 How long is the longest line?

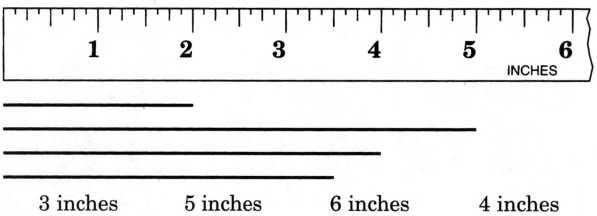

3 inches   5 inches   6 inches   4 inches

Ⓕ   Ⓖ   Ⓗ   Ⓙ

GO ▷

Look at the calendar.

NOVEMBER						
SUN	MON	TUE	WED	THU	FRI	SAT
					1	2
3	4	5	6	7	8	9
10	11	12	13	14	15	16
17	18	19	20	21	22	23
24	25	26	27	28	29	30

11 Thanksgiving is the fourth Thursday in November. What is that date?

Nov. 28   Ⓐ   Nov. 27   Ⓑ   Nov. 22   Ⓒ   Nov. 21   Ⓓ

12 Zeke started studying for his math test on Nov. 4. The test will be given on the following Friday. What date is that?

Nov. 3   Ⓕ   Nov. 4   Ⓖ   Nov. 15   Ⓗ   Nov. 8   Ⓙ

13 What day of the week is November 18?

Sunday   Ⓐ   Monday   Ⓑ   Tuesday   Ⓒ   Wednesday   Ⓓ

Look at the chart. It shows the test scores of four students.

	Math	Science	Spelling
Sheena	88	92	94
Bruce	86	93	90
Alyce	92	92	96
John	92	89	95

14 Which student has the highest test score?

John   Ⓕ   Alyce   Ⓖ   Bruce   Ⓗ   Sheena   Ⓙ

15 What is the difference between John's spelling score and his science score?

3 points   Ⓐ   4 points   Ⓑ   6 points   Ⓒ   95 points   Ⓓ

GO ⟩

Directions: Look at the graph. Then choose the best answer to the question.

NUMBER OF JARS PICKED

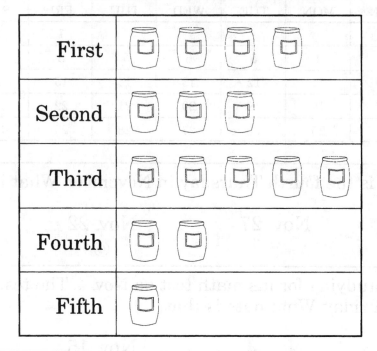

16   Which grade picked three jars of berries?

Second	First	Fourth	Third
Ⓕ	Ⓖ	Ⓗ	Ⓙ

17   How many jars did the students in all the grades pick together?

4	7	9	5
Ⓐ	Ⓑ	Ⓒ	Ⓓ

18   How many more jars did the third grade pick than the second grade?

1	3	5	2
Ⓕ	Ⓖ	Ⓗ	Ⓙ

19   Which shape is the same as the gray shape, only smaller?

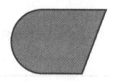   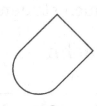

Ⓐ   Ⓑ   Ⓒ

STOP

Answer Key

Reading
Unit 1,
Word Analysis
Lesson 1–pg. 12

A	A
1	D
2	H
3	D
4	F
5	B
6	F

Lesson 2–pg. 13

A	B
1	C
2	F
3	D
4	H

Lesson 3–pg. 14

A	A
B	J
C	C
1	B
2	F
3	D
4	G
5	C

Lesson 4–pg. 15

A	B
1	C
2	F
3	B

Lesson 5–pg. 16

A	A
B	H
1	C
2	G
3	D
4	F
5	D
6	G

Lesson 6–pg. 17

A	C
B	F
1	B
2	F
3	D
4	G
5	C

Lesson 7–pg. 18

A	B
B	H

C	A
D	G
1	B
2	F
3	C
4	G
5	C
6	G
7	C
8	G
9	C
10	G
11	C
12	F

Lesson 8–pgs. 19–21

A	B
B	J
C	C
D	F
1	C
2	G
3	A
4	H
5	B
6	F
7	D
8	G
9	C
10	J
11	C
12	F
13	B
14	F
15	B
16	F
17	C
18	G

Unit 2,
Vocabulary
Lesson 9–pg. 22

A	C
1	B
2	G
3	C
4	F

Lesson 10–pg. 23

A	C
B	F
1	B
2	F
3	C
4	F
5	B

6	F
7	C
8	G
9	C
10	G
11	C
12	F

Lesson 11–pg. 24

A	A
B	H
1	D
2	G
3	A
4	J
5	C
6	G
7	D

Lesson 12–pg. 25

A	A
B	F
1	B
2	H
3	D
4	G
5	C
6	F

Lesson 13–pg. 26

A	A
B	F
1	D
2	H
3	A
4	G
5	A
6	J

Lesson 14–pg. 27

A	A
B	J
1	C
2	G
3	B
4	H

Lesson 15–pgs. 28–31

A	C
B	G
C	A
1	B
2	H
3	A
4	F
5	A

6	H
7	C
8	G
9	A
10	H
11	C
12	G
13	A
14	G
15	C
16	F
17	B
18	F
19	D
20	H
21	C
22	G
23	A
24	F
25	D
26	H
27	A
28	G
29	B
30	J
31	A
32	F

Unit 3,
Reading Comprehension
Lesson 16–pg. 32

A	C
1	A
2	H
3	B

Lesson 17–pg. 33

A	B
1	A
2	H
3	B
4	H

Lesson 18–pg. 34

A	B
B	H
1	A
2	G
3	A
4	H

Lesson 19–pgs. 35–38

A	B
1	A
2	H
3	A

4	H
5	B
6	G
7	A
8	H
9	A
10	J
11	A
12	H
13	B

Lesson 20–pgs. 39–41

A	A
1	B
2	H
3	B
4	G
5	A
6	G
7	C
8	G
9	A
10	H

**Test Practice,
Part 1–pgs. 44–47**

A	A
B	G
C	A
D	F
1	D
2	F
3	D
4	H
5	B
6	G
7	C
8	F
9	C
10	J
11	B
12	J
13	B
14	F
15	C
16	G
17	D
18	F
19	C
20	G
21	B
22	F
23	C
24	F

Part 2–pgs. 48–51

A	C
B	G
C	A
1	A
2	H

3	B
4	F
5	C
6	J
7	A
8	H
9	C
10	G
11	A
12	H
13	C
14	G
15	A
16	G
17	C
18	F
19	A
20	H
21	B
22	J
23	C
24	G
25	C
26	F
27	D
28	J
29	B
30	H
31	A

Part 3–pgs. 52–58

A	B
B	H
C	B
D	F
E	B
1	C
2	F
3	C
4	G
5	A
6	H
7	B
8	H
9	B
10	F
11	C
12	F
13	B
14	F
15	C
16	G
17	C
18	H
19	B
20	G
21	A
22	F
23	C
24	G
25	A

26	F
27	D
28	G
29	D

**Language
Unit 1, Listening
Lesson 1–pgs. 60–62**

A	A
B	G
C	C
1	B
2	H
3	A
4	F
5	A
6	H
7	B
8	H
9	A
10	G
11	B
12	F
13	C

Lesson 2–pgs. 63–64

A	A
1	A
2	H
3	B
4	G
5	A
6	H
7	B

Lesson 3–pgs. 65–67

E1	C
E2	G
E3	A
1	C
2	F
3	B
4	H
5	A
6	H
7	B
8	H
9	B
10	H
11	B
12	F
13	B
14	H

Lesson 4–pgs. 68–69

A	B
B	H
C	C
D	G
E	A
1	B

2	F
3	C
4	G
5	A
6	H
7	B
8	H
9	A
10	F
11	C

Lesson 5–pgs. 70–71

A	B
B	H
C	B
D	F
E	C
1	A
2	G
3	C
4	G
5	A
6	F
7	C
8	G
9	A
10	H
11	B

Lesson 6–pg. 72

A	B
B	F
1	C
2	F
3	B
4	G
5	C
6	F

Lesson 7–pgs. 73–77

E1	A
E2	H
E3	B
E4	F
E5	B
E6	H
E7	B
E8	F
E9	C
E10	G
E11	C
E12	G
1	B
2	G
3	C
4	F
5	C
6	F
7	A
8	H
9	A

10	H		2	G		10	F		9	A
11	B		3	C		11	C		10	H
12	F		4	F		12	G		11	A
13	B		5	A		13	C		12	H
14	G		6	G		14	H		13	B
15	A		7	C		15	B		14	F
16	F		8	F		16	F			
17	B		9	B					**Part 2–pgs. 98–101**	
18	G		10	F		**Lesson 14–pgs. 89–90**			E1	A
19	B		11	B		E1	C		E2	H
20	F		12	H		E2	F		E3	C
21	A					E3	B		E4	H
22	H		**Lesson 11–pg. 83**			E4	H		E5	A
23	A		A	C		1	A		E6	H
24	G		1	B		2	H		E7	B
25	A		2	H		3	B		E8	F
26	H		3	A		4	F		E9	C
27	B		4	G		5	B		E10	G
28	H					6	G		E11	A
29	B		**Lesson 12–pgs. 84–86**			7	C		1	B
30	F		E1	C		8	F		2	F
31	A		E2	G		9	C		3	C
32	H		E3	B		10	G		4	F
			E4	H		11	C		5	C
Unit 3			E5	A		12	F		6	G
Lesson 8–pgs. 78–79			E6	H		13	A		7	A
A	C		1	B		14	G		8	H
B	H		2	F		15	C		9	C
C	A		3	C		16	F		10	G
D	H		4	H		17	B		11	A
1	B		5	A		18	H		12	G
2	F		6	H					13	A
3	C		7	B		**Unit 5**			14	G
4	F		8	F		**Lesson 15–pg. 91**			15	C
5	C		9	C		A	C		16	H
6	G		10	F		1	C		17	B
7	B		11	B		2	G		18	H
8	F		12	F		3	A		19	A
9	C		13	C		4	H		20	F
10	G		14	G					21	C
11	A		15	C		**Lesson 16–pg. 92**			22	H
12	H		16	F		E1	B		23	A
13	B		17	B		1	B		24	G
14	H		18	G		2	F		25	B
			19	A		3	C			
Lesson 9–pg. 80						4	F		**Part 3–pgs. 102–103**	
A	A		**Unit 4**			5	C		E1	C
B	H		**Lesson 13–pgs. 87–88**						E2	G
1	C		A	B		**Test Practice,**			E3	B
2	G		B	F		**Part 1–pgs. 95–97**			E4	H
3	C		C	A		E1	B		1	B
4	F		D	G		E2	H		2	F
5	A		1	C		E3	B		3	C
6	H		2	F		1	A		4	F
			3	B		2	H		5	A
Lesson 10–pgs. 81–82			4	F		3	B		6	H
A	B		5	B		4	G		7	B
B	H		6	H		5	C		8	H
C	B		7	C		6	F		9	C
D	H		8	F		7	C		10	F
1	C		9	B		8	G		11	B

12	H
13	B

Part 4–pgs. 104–105

E1	C
E2	F
E3	B
E4	F
1	A
2	H
3	B
4	G
5	C
6	G
7	A
8	H
9	B
10	F
11	C
12	F
13	B
14	F
15	C
16	F
17	B
18	F

Part 5–pg. 106

E1	B
1	C
2	F
3	B
4	H
5	A

Math
Unit 1, Concepts
Lesson 1–pgs. 108–109

A	B
1	D
2	F
3	B
4	H
5	C
6	F
7	G
8	J

Lesson 2–pgs. 110–111

A	B
1	C
2	F
3	B
4	G
5	C
6	J
7	A
8	G
9	D

Lesson 3–pgs. 112–113

A	B
1	C
2	F
3	B
4	F
5	B
6	G
7	A
8	J
9	C
10	F

Lesson 4–pgs. 114–115

A	A
1	B
2	J
3	A
4	G
5	B
6	H
7	A
8	H

Lesson 5–pgs. 116–119

E1	D
1	C
2	H
3	A
4	G
5	A
6	G
7	D
8	H
9	A
10	F
11	B
12	H
13	B
14	G
15	A
16	G
17	C
18	H
19	C
20	G
21	B

Unit 2
Lesson 6–pgs. 120–121

A	C
B	J
1	D
2	F
3	C
4	G
5	B
6	F
7	C
8	J
9	C
10	G
11	D
12	F
13	B
14	F

Lesson 7–pgs. 122–123

A	D
B	F
1	A
2	J
3	B
4	H
5	D
6	G
7	C
8	F
9	B
10	G
11	C
12	H
13	D
14	F

Lesson 8–pgs. 124–125

E1	D
E2	F
1	A
2	H
3	B
4	J
5	A
6	H
7	A
8	G
9	C
10	H
11	C
12	F
13	B
14	J
15	B
16	J
17	C
18	F

Unit 3
Lesson 9–pgs. 126–129

A	B
1	D
2	G
3	A
4	G
5	D
6	F
7	B
8	F
9	A
10	H
11	C
12	J
13	D
14	F
15	B
16	H
17	C
18	J

Lesson 10–pgs. 130–133

A	B
1	B
2	F
3	C
4	G
5	D
6	H
7	A
8	F
9	D
10	G
11	D
12	H
13	C
14	F
15	C

Lesson 11–pgs. 134–137

A	D
1	B
2	H
3	A
4	H
5	B
6	F
7	D
8	F
9	C
10	J
11	B
12	H
13	A
14	J
15	B

Lesson 12–pgs. 138–141

E1	B
1	A
2	G
3	D
4	H
5	B
6	J
7	A
8	H
9	D
10	J
11	A
12	F
13	D

14	H	13	C	9	D	1	D
15	B	14	F	10	H	2	G
16	H	15	C	11	B	3	D
17	D	16	J	12	F	4	G
18	F	17	A	13	D	5	B
		18	G	14	H	6	F
		19	A	15	A	7	C
		20	H	16	H	8	F
		21	C	17	B	9	A
				18	H	10	G

**Test Practice,
Part 1–pgs. 144–147**

E1	A			19	A	11	A
1	C			20	H	12	J
2	F	**Part 2–pgs. 148–150**		21	D	13	B
3	C	E1	D	22	G	14	G
4	G	E2	J	23	D	15	C
5	B	1	C	24	H	16	F
6	J	2	F	25	B	17	B
7	C	3	D	26	F	18	J
8	F	4	G			19	B
9	B	5	D				
10	F	6	G	**Part 3–pgs. 151–154**			
11	C	7	A	E1	C		
12	F	8	G				

Reading Progress Chart

Circle your score for each lesson. Connect your scores to see how well you are doing.

Unit	Lesson	Scores (top to bottom)
Unit 1	Lesson 1	6, 5, 4, 3, 2, 1
	Lesson 2	4, 3, 2, 1
	Lesson 3	5, 4, 3, 2, 1
	Lesson 4	3, 2, 1
	Lesson 5	6, 5, 4, 3, 2, 1
	Lesson 6	5, 4, 3, 2, 1
	Lesson 7	12, 11, 10, 9, 8, 7, 6, 5, 4, 3, 2, 1
	Lesson 8	18, 17, 16, 15, 14, 13, 12, 11, 10, 9, 8, 7, 6, 5, 4, 3, 2, 1
Unit 2	Lesson 9	4, 3, 2, 1
	Lesson 10	12, 11, 10, 9, 8, 7, 6, 5, 4, 3, 2, 1
	Lesson 11	7, 6, 5, 4, 3, 2, 1
	Lesson 12	6, 5, 4, 3, 2, 1
	Lesson 13	6, 5, 4, 3, 2, 1
	Lesson 14	4, 3, 2, 1
	Lesson 15	32, 31, 30, 29, 28, 27, 26, 25, 24, 23, 22, 21, 20, 19, 18, 17, 16, 15, 14, 13, 12, 11, 10, 9, 8, 7, 6, 5, 4, 3, 2, 1
Unit 3	Lesson 16	3, 2, 1
	Lesson 17	4, 3, 2, 1
	Lesson 18	4, 3, 2, 1
	Lesson 19	13, 12, 11, 10, 9, 8, 7, 6, 5, 4, 3, 2, 1
	Lesson 20	10, 9, 8, 7, 6, 5, 4, 3, 2, 1

Language Progress Chart

Circle your score for each lesson. Connect your scores to see how well you are doing.

Unit 1			Unit 2					Unit 3				Unit 4		Unit 5	
Lesson 1	Lesson 2	Lesson 3	Lesson 4	Lesson 5	Lesson 6	Lesson 7	Lesson 8	Lesson 9	Lesson 10	Lesson 11	Lesson 12	Lesson 13	Lesson 14	Lesson 15	Lesson 16
						32									
						31									
						30									
						29									
						28									
						27									
						26									
						25									
						24									
						23									
						22									
						21									
						20									
						19					19				
						18					18		18		
						17					17		17		
						16					16	16	16		
						15					15	15	15		
		14				14	14				14	14	14		
13		13				13	13				13	13	13		
12		12				12	12		12		12	12	12		
11		11	11	11		11	11		11		11	11	11		
10		10	10	10		10	10		10		10	10	10		
9		9	9	9		9	9		9		9	9	9		
8		8	8	8		8	8		8		8	8	8		
7	7	7	7	7		7	7		7		7	7	7		
6	6	6	6	6	6	6	6	6	6		6	6	6		
5	5	5	5	5	5	5	5	5	5		5	5	5		5
4	4	4	4	4	4	4	4	4	4	4	4	4	4	4	4
3	3	3	3	3	3	3	3	3	3	3	3	3	3	3	3
2	2	2	2	2	2	2	2	2	2	2	2	2	2	2	2
1	1	1	1	1	1	1	1	1	1	1	1	1	1	1	1

Math Progress Chart

Circle your score for each lesson. Connect your scores to see how well you are doing.

Unit 1				Unit 2			Unit 3				
Lesson 1	Lesson 2	Lesson 3	Lesson 4	Lesson 5	Lesson 6	Lesson 7	Lesson 8	Lesson 9	Lesson 10	Lesson 11	Lesson 12
8	9	10	8	21	14	14	18	18	15	15	18
7	8	9	7	20	13	13	17	17	14	14	17
6	7	8	6	19	12	12	16	16	13	13	16
5	6	7	5	18	11	11	15	15	12	12	15
4	5	6	4	17	10	10	14	14	11	11	14
3	4	5	3	16	9	9	13	13	10	10	13
2	3	4	2	15	8	8	12	12	9	9	12
1	2	3	1	14	7	7	11	11	8	8	11
	1	2		13	6	6	10	10	7	7	10
		1		12	5	5	9	9	6	6	9
				11	4	4	8	8	5	5	8
				10	3	3	7	7	4	4	7
				9	2	2	6	6	3	3	6
				8	1	1	5	5	2	2	5
				7			4	4	1	1	4
				6			3	3			3
				5			2	2			2
				4			1	1			1
				3							
				2							
				1							

STUDENT NOTES

STUDENT NOTES

STUDENT NOTES

STUDENT NOTES

STUDENT NOTES

STUDENT NOTES